Letters of

GUSTAF NORDENSKIÖLD

Written in the Year 1891
and
Articles from the Journals
Ymer
and
Photographic Times

The SS "*Waesland*."
Gustaf Nordenskiöld arrived in the United States aboard this ship
at New York on May 26, 1891.
Photo courtesy the Peabody Museum of Salem. Salem, Mass.

Letters of

GUSTAF NORDENSKIÖLD

Written in the Year 1891
and
Articles from the Journals
Ymer
and
Photographic Times

Edited by
Irving L. Diamond
and
Daniel M. Olson

Translated from Swedish by
Daniel M. Olson

MESA VERDE MUSEUM ASSOCIATION, INC.
Mesa Verde National Park, Colorado

1991

Published by the
The Mesa Verde Museum Association, Inc.
Mesa Verde National Park, Colorado 81330
Copyright 1991

Library of Congress Catalog Number: 91-60270
ISBN 0-937-06216-2

The photograph of Gustaf Nordenskiöld on the front cover was
made in Durango, Colorado in 1891 at the Gonner & Hurd
Studio. It is used here courtesy of the Arrhenius and
Nordenskiöld families.

The cover layout was prepared by Sandi Nelson.

This book is printed on acid-free recycled paper.

CONTENTS

PAGE

Introduction: Robert C. Heyder, Superintendent,   9
Mesa Verde National Park.

Editors' Comments   11

The Nordenskiöld Letters

1. Florence, Italy, 2 March 1891 to his Mother.   15
2. Antwerp, Belgium, 15 May 1891 to his Mother.   16
3. "S.S. *Waesland*", 27 May 1891 to his Mother.   17
4. Jersey City, N. J. 29 May 1891 to his Father.   18
5. Niagara Falls, N. Y. 30 May 1891 to his Mother.   19
6. Washington, D. C. 2 June 1891 to his Father.   20
7. Philadelphia, 3 June 1891 to his Father.   21
8. Philadelphia, 3 June 1891 to his Mother.   22
9. Charleston, S. C. 10 June 1891 to his Father.   23
10. Charleston, S. C. 10 June 1891 to his Mother.   24
11. Mammoth Cave, Kentucky 19 June 1891 to his Father.   25
12. Chicago, Ill., Midsummer's Day (24 June),1891 to his Father.   26
13. Denver, 27 June 1891 to his Mother.   27
14. Denver, 30 June 1891 to his Father.   28
15. Mancos Valley, 2 July 1891 to his Father.   29
16. Mancos Valley, 3 July 1891 to his Father.   32
17. Mancos, Montezuma County, Colorado, 15 July 1891 to his Mother.   33

18. Mancos Valley, 18 July 1891   34
    to "Ka" (Karl), a cousin.

19. Durango, Colo., 29 July 1891 to his Father.   37

20. Mancos, 31 July 1891 to his Mother.   40

21. Mancos, 14 August 1891 to his Father.   43

22. Mancos, Montezuma County,Colorado,   44
    15 August 1891 to his Mother.

23. Navajo Cañon, 18 August 1891 to his Father.   45

24. Navajo Cañon, 23 August 1891 to his Father.   45

25. Mancos, 29 August 1891 to his Mother.   48

26. Mancos, 29 August 1891 to his Father.   49

27. Mancos, 30 August 1891 to "B. B."   49

28. Mancos, 31 August 1891 to his Father.   50

29. Mancos, 9 September 1891 to his Father.   51

30. Mancos, 16 September 1891 to his Father.   52

31. Durango, Colorado, 17 September 1891   53
    to his Father.

32. Mancos, 19 September 1891 to his Father.   53

33. Durango, Colorado 27 September 1891   54
    to his Father.

34. Durango, Colorado 30 September 1891   56
    to his Father.

35. Durango, 3 October 1891. Postscript   57
    dated 5 October to his Father.

36. Durango, Colorado, 7 October 1891 to his Father.   59

37. Durango, Colorado, 21 October 1891 to his Father.   59

38. Durango, Colorado, 22 October 1891 to his Father.   61

39. Mancos, 23 October 1891 to to his Mother.   62

40. Mancos, 23 October 1891 to "Ka" (Karl), a cousin.   63

41. Mancos, 1 November 1891 to his Father.   64

Articles by Nordenskiöld

"On some remarkable ruins in Southwestern
Colorado," *Ymer* , 1892.   69

'The development of the meander-pattern among
Colorado's cliff dwellers," *Ymer*, 1892.   83

'The Photography of Snow Flakes",
The Photographic Times, February 1895.   91

Bibliography   97

Introduction

One cannot be associated with Mesa Verde National Park very long without hearing the name Nordenskiöld. Gustaf Erik Nordenskiöld was on a trip around the world when he visited the ruins of Mesa Verde in July 1891. A visit of a few days stretched into six months and a great deal of field work, excavating and photographing select ruins of the Mesa Verde. This work led to Nordenskiöld's great volume, *The Cliff Dwellers of the Mesa Verde*, which was published first in Swedish and then in English. His work is considered by many to be the cornerstone of Southwestern archeology.

This volume, The Letters of Gustaf Nordenskiöld, is most timely now to help celebrate the centennial of Nordenskiöld's work here at Mesa Verde. The publication of his letters home to Sweden gives us great insight into the young man who produced so much in his short life. In reading this volume of his letters, two articles on his excavation at Mesa Verde and work in microphotography of snowflakes, one finds a man of broad ranging interest.

Irving L. Diamond has spent many devoted hours to bring this material together for the first time. Daniel M. Olson translated all of the Swedish material and served as co-editor. I am sure that it will renew interest in both Nordenskiöld and the Wetherills, as they have left their mark on this culturally rich land of the American Southwest. This book will take its place as an important addition to the history of Southwestern archeology.

Robert C. Heyder
Superintendent
Mesa Verde National Park
January 28, 1991

Editors' Comments

"The summer of 1891 I passed in Colorado, engaged upon investigations of the remarkable cliff-dwellings scattered in the cañons of an extensive plateau, the Mesa Verde, in the southwest of the State." Thus Gustaf Nordenskiöld, the author of the letters presented here one hundred years after they were written, summed up his sojourn in the Mesa Verde. Nordenskiöld arrived in Colorado on his way to San Francisco and Yokohama, Japan. He decided, however, to remain in the Mesa Verde to study this mysterious locale. We might surmise that he saw what the character Tom Outland "saw" in Willa Cather's novel *The Professor's House*, when he viewed a cliff dwelling for the first time:

> Far up above me, a thousand feet or so, set in a great cavern, in the face of the cliff, I saw a little city of stone, asleep. It was still as sculpture. ...A fringe of cedars grew along the edge of the cavern, like a garden. ...I knew at once that I had come upon the city of some extinct civilization ...guarded by the cliffs and the river and the desert.

Gustaf Nordenskiöld was an educated twenty-two year old when he arrived in the United States on May 26, 1891. Gustaf was born in 1868 in Stockholm. Throughout his early school years Gustaf exhibited a love for learning and science. His father, A. E. Nordenskiöld, saw to it that his children were proficient in areas other than schooling. Summers were spent at the family's country home at Dalbyö in Northern Sweden.

Gustaf was trained in chemistry and mineralogy at the University of Uppsala. In 1890, he was a member of a geological expedition to Spitsbergen, an island near the Arctic Ocean. During this expedition, he contracted tuberculosis, the disease which would claim his life in 1895.

A. E. Nordenskiöld, Gustaf's father, was head of the Mineralogical Department at the Swedish Academy of Science, and was world-famous for his exploits as a polar explorer. His book, *The Voyage of the Vega*, which is mentioned in these letters describes his circumnavigation of Asia and Europe. He was also a collector of maps and globes of the sixteenth and seventeenth centuries; Japanese literature; and Eskimo artifacts from Port Clarence, Alaska.

In these letters, we meet Gustaf in Florence, Italy, near the beginning of his "grand tour." He had travelled to Italy by way of Berlin, where he had sought treatment for his tuberculosis.

During his stay at the Mesa Verde, Gustaf made his home with the family of Benjamin K. Wetherill, a rancher in Mancos, Colorado. Richard Wetherill, son of Benjamin Wetherill, and his brother-in-law, Charlie Mason, had discovered Cliff Palace and other cliff-dwellings in the cañons of the Mesa Verde in 1888.

Many persons mentioned in these letters have not been identified. Briefly, some of the others are: James D. Dana, (1813-1895), a geologist; George C. Brush (born 1831), a mineralogist; O. C. Marsh (1831-1899), paleontologist; and Samuel L. Pennfield (1856-1906), a mineralogist. The Dr. [Fritjof] Antell mentioned in the letter from Paris dated May 15, 1891, would a few years later purchase the collection of Anasazi artifacts which Gustaf assembled in Colorado. Dr. Antell eventually made a gift of this collection to the Finnish nation. Its home is the National Museum of Finland in Helsinki.

Gustaf writes about his arrest in Durango, Colorado on September 17, 1891 when he attempted to send his collection home to Sweden. As he relates in a postscript dated October 5, 1891, he was released from a bail of one-thousand dollars. He was then allowed to ship his collection home.

The judge in his case was Cyrus F. Newcomb. Judge Newcomb arrived in Durango in 1887 after living in ten states from Massachusetts, where he was born, to California. By then he had worked in hotels, as a travelling salesman, in ore refining, as deputy mayor of Del Norte, Colorado and as a deputy revenue collector.

Adair Wilson was the attorney Gustaf hired to assist him with the United States court. Mr. Ritter, a citizen of Durango, whom Gustaf had come to know, wrote several letters to United States officials in defense of Gustaf's work in the Mesa Verde.

12

The articles Gustaf talks of sending home were published in a Stockholm newspaper. Later, he published them as a book entitled *From the Far West: Memories from America.*

Most of the letters presented here have never been published before. Those dated May 27 (Number 3), May 30 (Number 5), June 3 (to his Mother, Number 7) , June 10 (to his father, Number 10), June 27 (Number 13), and July 2 (Number 15) were excerpted in the very fine volume *Stones Speak and Waters Sing,* based upon a memoir by Olof Arrhenius, son-in-law of Gustaf Nordenskiöld. Robert H. Lister and Florence Lister provided extensive enhancements for publication of this book.

The letters numbered 4, 6, 7, 8, 9, 11, 12 , 14, 16, 17, 18, 19, 21, 22, 23, 24, 26, 28, 29, 31, 32, 33, 34, 35, 36, 37, 38, and 41, are from the archives of the Nordenskiöld family through the courtesy of Gustaf Arrhenius, grandson of Gustaf Nordenskiöld.

Letters numbered 1, 2, 3, 5, 10, 13, 15, 20, 25, 27, 30, 39, and 40 are from the Royal Library in Stockholm. The director, Professor Tore Frängsmyr, has graciously granted permission for publication. We wish to thank Mr. Esko Rahikainen, Librarian at the University of Helsinki Library, for guiding us to the letters at the Royal Library.

Our aim has been to retain the style of speech used by Nordenskiöld in forms of address. Square brackets are used to mark editors' interpolations. *Sic* in square brackets denotes odd or erroneous phrases contained in the original letters.

All translations were made by Daniel M. Olson. His work was funded by the Swedish-American Historical Society, Chicago. Timothy Johnson, archivist for the Society, provided essential assistance.

Robert C. Heyder, Superintendent of Mesa Verde National Park, was enthusiastic in his encouragement to us in the preparation of these letters for publication. Art Hutchinson, National Park Ranger, and Mona Hutchinson offered assistance in many ways. We thank the Mesa Verde Museum Association, Inc. for financing the printing and distribution of this volume; in particular Rovilla Ellis, Executive Director.

This photograph is of Gustaf Nordenskiöld and two unidentified women. It was probably taken in Italy before Nordenskiöld came to America. He is wearing a student cap of the type mentioned in letter *No. 1 to his Mother.* From the collection of Nordenskiöld photographs at the National Museum of Finland, Helsinki

No. 1 to his Mother

Florence, 2 March 1891

Dear Mother

I wrote my last letter from Munich. The following morning I travelled on, and after a beautiful and interesting journey through the Alps I found myself in Verona. I stayed in Verona for one day and saw the magnificent Roman amphitheater there, as well as a number of other beautiful things. I arrived in Florence yesterday afternoon, and have seen so many beautiful sites that I am quite dizzy. Tomorrow I shall visit two more galleries, and then leave for Rome. I should be in Rome by 11:00 tomorrow evening. The weather here is beautiful, we have had nothing but sunshine. I apologize to you people way up in the chilly North, who still have to wear winter coats and freeze in below-zero weather. They know nothing of our Swedish tile stoves [*kakelugnar*] here, and it is usually warmer outside than in. The room I had in Verona was really cold. However, there was a sort of a miniature tile stove there. Unfortunately, it did not throw out any heat at all, even though I stuffed 3 *lira* worth of firewood into it.

In Munich I visited an art gallery. I even got to hear Professor Groth speak, although he was so hoarse from the recent foul weather that the audience became short of attention. I got to look at many of his beautiful mineral samples. He had some magnificent examples from the Alps. Professor Groth asked me to greet Father, and tell him that he would like to exchange duplicate samples of minerals. Please tell Father about this. Tell him also that I have finished writing my article about coprolite, and that I'll send it from Rome, once I've had the chance to settle down there. I'll write more from Rome as soon as I've collected my mail.

Greetings to Father, Erland, and Anna from your devoted Gustaf

P.S. It is getting much too warm for me to wear my top hat. I would very much appreciate it if you could send a Swedish student cap to me here in Rome. You could also send my razors and other shaving gear. I need the razors that say "Eskilstuna" right on the blades. If Lisa is still working for you, she will know where the other shaving articles are.

15

No. 2 to his Mother

Antwerp, 15 May 1891

Dear Mother

I arrived here today after spending a week in Paris with Dr. Antell, who was very kind to me. He even let me stay in his house. Since I am leaving early tomorrow morning, I thought it best to scribble out a few lines to you. I have sent a knapsack, and a top hat in its carrying case to Stockholm. Please do not unpack the former; let it be until I get home. I got in from Paris yesterday evening. Since you and Anna both know Paris, I do not need to describe its beauties for you (I was able to see both salons). You can be sure that my week there was over and done with before I knew it, and since my ticket to New York had already been bought, I had to leave. I had dinner with Descloiseau, who naturally asked that I greet both Mother and Father. I spent one day together with the Canadian travelling companion I met in Naples, Mr. John Ball, and his sister Miss Ball. One evening we also went to the Opera Comique together.

Antwerp is a boring city, and the people here look boring. The best thing about this town is a rather noteworthy cathedral.

I shall write more once I've crossed the Atlantic. I probably won't have opportunity to write until then. Thank you for your letter of the 30th of April, which I received today. Do not expect another letter from me until the end of June. As far as what my mailing address will be, it is difficult to say. For now it would probably be best to send my mail to the New York Swedish Consulate. I'll probably stay in that city only a few days, but I can leave my forwarding address with them. Farewell for now. Greet Anna and Erland from me, and thank Anna for her letter.

From Mother's devoted Gustaf

No. 3 to his Mother

On board the "S.S. Waesland"
[Mailed from] New York, 27 May 1891

Dearest Mother

I have arrived safely in New York after a comparatively good voyage. There were only several days when the wind blew hard, and I did experience some mild seasickness. Otherwise, the trip was pleasant, and took 11 days from Antwerp. The passengers on board were mostly Yankees. There were 15 passengers in first class, including a watchmaker from Colorado who had been in Switzerland to learn more about his field, a cattle-range man, that is, a horse dealer or something similar, from San Francisco, and a musician from Chicago who had been studying in Munich. There was a German who the first time he came to America, had fled from his parents and travelled in third class, but had now gotten a wife, and seemed to have made his fortune here in the West. There were also two young American women who had been in Paris to study and practice painting. One of them, extremely beautiful, with golden blond hair and dark eyes, had completely entranced the ship's doctor.

One day after another has disappeared in conversation, games, naps and lazing about. All of these people, brought together by chance for 11 days in the cramped accommodations on board the *Waesland* have become fast friends, but are now to be spread to the four corners of the earth once again.

I am expecting to see much of interest during my time in America. As soon as I have read the letters which I hope are waiting for me in New York, I shall write to tell you of my travel plans, and give a forwarding address. If you write to me immediately at the Chicago Swedish Consulate, you'll probably reach me.

Many greetings to everyone at home from

Mother's devoted Gustaf

No. 4 to his Father

Taylor's Hotel, Jersey City, N.J., 29 May 1891

I have spent a few days in New York, waiting in vain for a letter from you, Father. This evening I shall be travelling to Niagara, and from there on to Washington, where I have directed the consul to send my letters. Some cutbacks in the railways are expected, according to an agreement between the different rail companies, to be directed at none other than the employees themselves. From Washington, I will travel down to South Carolina, and then up to Chicago. I have seen the Museum of Natural History here in New York. It is beautiful and well organized, although not especially large. The only other attraction I've seen has been a gallery of Vereshchagin's paintings. I do not have much time to write now, the train is leaving soon. I shall send in my first newspaper letter once I have visited Mammoth Cave in Kentucky, and the phosphate mines in South Carolina. In many ways, it is uncomfortably expensive here. To have my baggage transported to the station, it cost $1.50, which is more than 5 Swedish crowns.

I shall be passing through the Green River Valley; I wonder if one couldn't obtain some of those Tertiary bones, such as Marsh found there? My funds will last until San Francisco, but it would be good to have a little more sent over, in case some unforeseen event should come about. Could Pappa send over 100 dollars more, to the address "Swedish Consulate, Chicago?" I will probably already have left that city by then, but will leave orders with the consul to send the money to some specific place in the West. However, this won't be absolutely necessary if Pappa thinks it is too much. Perhaps after my return home I shall be able to publish these travel reports, with increased detail, in book form, to help out a little [with the expenses]. I shall write more at the first opportunity. I have a long way to go to the railway station.

Greet everyone there at home from Pappa's devoted Gustaf.

No. 5 to his Mother

Western Hotel, Niagara Falls, N.Y., 30 May 1891

Dear Mother

Thank you for the two letters you sent from Dalbyö. I received them soon after stepping ashore in New York. New York is a terribly unpleasant and dirty city, although it is somewhat better when one gets away from downtown. Thanks to the "elevated railroad," one can get into this huge city from two different points. Transportation here is better than in any other city I have been in.

Yesterday, I visited New Haven and saw the Peabody Museum. There I met Dana, Brush, Marsh, and Pennfield, who all send greetings to Father. Marsh himself showed me his collection of fossil bones, the most fantastic and interesting items. That night I went directly from New Haven to Niagara. As Mother herself knows how beautiful it is there, there is no need for me to give a description.

I will not be visiting Boston or Philadelphia, as I do not have time. Please write and tell me when my knapsack arrives from Antwerp. I am anxious to hear that it gets there safely, for it contains the journal I kept during the Spitsbergen expedition.

This evening I travel on to Washington, where I hope to find those long-awaited letters from Father. I'll write again from there. Greet Pappa and my siblings from

Your devoted Gustaf

No. 6 to his Father

Department of the Interior, United States Geological Survey, Washington, D.C.,
2 June 1891

Just a few lines to report that I received many letters today, among them the one which I was waiting for from Pappa. As a result, I will be travelling up to Philadelphia and shall look for Cassatt. Thereafter, I shall go down to South Carolina and Florida. If I am able to get an open-ended railway pass, it will be unnecessary to send the 100 dollars which I mentioned in the last letter. Even if I do not get the pass, I think that I can do without the money. I had intended to use it for a trip to the mines in Colorado, where I hope to find some good mineral samples. I made acquaintance with several geologists at the U. S. Geological Survey. They have been very obliging and friendly, and have given me many valuable addresses and recommendations for Colorado, Florida, South Carolina, etc. I received the announcement of Anna's engagement through Secretary Beck-Friis. Of course, it took me completely by surprise, as I was not at all prepared to hear of it. I shall write again tomorrow from Philadelphia, when I have looked up Mr. Cassatt. It will also be not at all unpleasant to be able to view Mr. Bement's celebrated collection of minerals. In the Consul's receiving room yesterday, I unexpectedly met Lindström's friend, the engraver Mr. Westergren, or Westerberg. He did not recognize me, but I knew immediately that I had seen the man before. He asked me to greet Mr. Lindström. It is already unbearably hot here. My health is still the best possible. Any letters you might send before the 20th of June should reach me in Denver at this address: Swedish Consulate, Denver, Colorado, U.S.A. After that, San Francisco, where I will await the advance of money. Greet everyone at home from me. I shall write more tomorrow.

Father's devoted Gustaf

[Note written in the margin of p. 1 of this letter -Ed.]
Philadelphia, 3 June. Have deposited the money. Was invited to dinner at the Cassatts'. Please congratulate Anna and her fiancé on their engagement on my behalf. Will write more tomorrow, have no time now.

No. 7 to his Father

Reese House, Philadelphia, 3 June, 1891

Pappa I have not succeeded in obtaining a discount as of yet. Shall try again in Chicago. Now I travel down to see the phosphate in both South Carolina and Florida. I fear that my purse is growing thin, and if I am to be able to go to the mines in Colorado, I shall need the 100 dollars which I wrote about, and which I hope Pappa has already sent to Denver, Colorado. It would be good that a card or letter indicating whether the sum has been forwarded be sent to the San Francisco, Calif. Swedish Consulate, since it is possible that I might find it more suitable to travel directly to San Francisco from Yellowstone. In such a case, it would be useful to know when I can expect to pick up the money in Denver. At any rate, the money will reach me. I need only to write to the Consul. Of course, I reported already in my previous letter that the 100 dollars for the Florida trip had reached me.

Mr. Bement's collection of minerals in Philadelphia is probably the most beautiful single collection in existence. Many of his items are magnificent, especially those from America. He expressed a wish to obtain beautiful examples from Norway and Sweden, as he does not presently have much from our country. He promised to send some fine American examples in exchange. He is an amateur, lacking any deeper education. He is besides a wealthy businessman. If you should send anything to him, it should be items of quality. He especially loves beautiful crystals, and does not really concern himself with whether or not they are of an important type of mineral.

You met him in '76, and he asked me to send you his greetings. I believe that it would be favorable to make an exchange with him. His address:
Mr. Bement
1804 Spring Garden St.
Philadelphia, Pa. U.S.A.

Many greetings from your devoted Gustaf

No. 8 to his Mother

Reese House, Philadelphia, Pennsylvania, 3 June 1891

Dear Mother

Many thanks for your last letter. It reached me in Washington, where I spent two days. I do not know if you have been there before. It is one of the most beautifully laid-out cities in the world. The Americans themselves are quite proud of it, and hold it to be the world's most beautiful city. I spent a pleasant evening there with Baron Beck-Friis, a young diplomat. I also met a number of geologists, who were all very friendly.

Last night, I traveled up to Philadelphia because of a letter I had received from Pappa. There I visited Mr. Cassatt, director (not president) of the Pennsylvania Railroad. The visit provided me with an excellent evening meal, but no reduction in ticket prices. It seems that I could have gotten a free travel pass for the Pennsylvania R.R.'s lines, but unfortunately, this is not the railroad I plan to travel on.

Tomorrow, I'll travel up to New York, and then on to Florida and South Carolina by steamer the same day. It is already uncomfortably hot here; in Florida, naturally, it will be seven times worse.

Here in Philadelphia, I have seen an extraordinarily beautiful mineral collection belonging to Mr. Bement. Otherwise, I have no news. I would like to hear a little more about my new future brother-in-law and his prospects for the future. Does he have money?

Write soon; address San Francisco California
Swedish Consulate, U.S.A.

Letters sent to that address will not reach me for a long time, but it is impossible for me to give a better one. I'll have to get along without letters for a few months. For letters written after this month, the address will be Yokohama Swedish Consulate.
Greetings to my brother, sister and Aunt Anna from Mother's devoted Gustaf

No. 9 to his Father

National House, Charleston, S.C., 10 June 1891

I have now visited the phosphate mines here, and shall send a report on them soon. It is difficult to compare them to those on Spitsbergen, for the outcroppings occur in such a different manner. The phosphate is found in masses from a few inches to several feet in diameter, mixed with about 50% sand. These masses occur in widely spread out layers, from 2 or 3 to 20 feet below the surface of the earth. The thickness of these layers is usually about one foot, but may vary from a few inches to 3 feet. The concentration of phosphoric acid is usually around 27 to 28%, but is sometimes quite a bit higher. In order to be saleable, the phosphate must be guaranteed to contain at least 25% phosphoric acid. Either today or tomorrow, I shall write a more complete report for you. I can hardly imagine that the outcroppings on Spitsbergen will be able to compete with these in ease of availability (the mining work here involves merely digging up the minerals), or in concentration of phosphoric acid, unless new analyses should give us different results. In addition, the phosphates in Florida, which have not yet been mined to any great extent, occur over a huge area. I shall give a report on these at a much later date. The remote location adds to the difficulties to be faced if mining is to be undertaken on Spitsbergen. Furthermore, the price of phosphate has recently gone down (7 to 8 dollars per ton).

I have sent off a box with some phosphate samples and a few bits of bone (which will prove to be worthless).

The next address where you will be able to reach me will be the Swedish Consulate in San Francisco.

Gustaf

No. 10 to his Mother

Charleston, South Carolina, 10 June 1891

Dear Mother

On the 5th of this month, I left New York on the steamer *Algonquin* and arrived in Charleston, S.C. The journey was rather boring, but with fine weather and warm, muggy winds from the south. As an experiment I travelled 2nd class, but I won't do it again. In Charleston, I visited some phosphate people to whom I had letters of introduction from Washington. Today and yesterday I have gone around and viewed the phosphate deposits; that was quite interesting.

The weather is very hot down here. I am on approximately the same latitude as Morocco in Africa. Date trees, oranges, lemons, magnolia, cedar, etc. grow everywhere here. There are some beautiful types of oaks and pines, including pitch pine, etc. The population is partly black and partly white, the former greater in number, the latter greater in wealth. The old bitterness towards the northern states since the Civil War still lives on among the people. I have visited with several families, all of them very hospitable. They have most likely been slave owners, and have made great profit from the free labor of their slaves. From here I intend to travel down to Florida, and then up to Chicago in about a week. Letters addressed to the San Francisco, Cal., Swedish Consulate should reach me when I arrive in that city. After that, the address to use will be the Swedish Consulate in Yokohama, Japan. If Anna wants some Japanese stamps, she should send me some Swedish and other European stamps; they will probably be worth money in Japan. Ask her to send them to Yokohama at once.

Greetings to Pappa, my brother, sister, and her fiancé, from Mother's devoted Gustaf

No. 11 to his Father

Mammoth Cave Hotel, Mammoth Cave, Kentucky, 19 June 1891

Yesterday and today, I have spent a total of 13 hours underground, and have covered 30 English miles (that equals 5 Swedish miles) in the fantastic passageways, arches, and rooms [of this cave]. I'll send a complete report of its wonders from Chicago, whence I am headed this evening. I'll also send a literary sketch of my Florida trip, and another about the phosphate sources there and in South Carolina, both of which are in the form of rough drafts. After having seen the phosphate sites in the latter state, I am convinced that an attempt to exploit the outcroppings on Spitsbergen would be comparatively difficult, even if the work there was not made even more troublesome by the remote location and the harsh climactic conditions. In any case, Pappa may decide for himself in this matter once my report arrives. I arrive in Chicago tomorrow morning at 11:00 a.m., and shall stay there only two days. From there, I'll travel to Colorado.

From Florida, I have sent you a small cigar box containing some bits of bone which I received as a gift from Dr. Shepard. He has also given me a box of excellent (according to him) phosphate samples from Florida (I don't know, as I haven't seen them myself). If you should feel as though you ought to send him a copy of *The Voyage of the Vega* or something similar in exchange, his address is Dr. Shepard, Chemical Director for the Dunbar Phosphate Co., Ocala, Florida. His father has been in Stockholm and has met you there. He was also an enthusiastic mineral collector. Soon it will be too hot here for me to write!

Greet everyone at home from Pappa's own devoted
Gustaf

No. 12 to his Father

Commercial Hotel, Chicago, Ill., Midsummer's Day (24 June), 1891

Along with this letter, I am sending a short article I have written on the phosphate mines in Florida. I have also included a few lines about Florida in general, which I intend to have published at the same time, to serve as an introduction. You'll also find a manuscript from Mammoth Cave in a very rough draft. It ought to be more interesting; at least, the cave itself was very grand and remarkable. I walked a total of 5 Swedish miles [35 American miles] in its depths. I don't really care to write so much about it now, since my report to you will be arriving in a few days.

I have received a few letters from Mamma, addressed to New York, and one from Anna quite soon after that. Letters sent up to and including the 1st of August should be addressed to me at the Yokohama Swedish Consulate, since there is one in existence there, although it is nothing more than a general delivery post office box! Tomorrow evening, I travel to Denver, Colorado, and from there to Pike's Peak. I hope to be able to get an open-ended ticket to that destination.

Please send me my articles once they are published. If they do not get published, please keep the manuscripts on my behalf, for I want to have them in the future. I hope the bones and phosphate samples I sent have arrived safely. Greet everyone there at home from

Father's devoted Gustaf

P.S. The day before yesterday, I saw Dr. A. Fraenkel, who examined me. He advised me to continue with a dose of 0.1 gram every week. Yesterday, I was given my first injection in 4 weeks. I experienced a mild reaction to it. Tomorrow I will receive 0.1 gram, and equally as much every week. There is no longer any difficulty in obtaining serum, so I shall get my own bottle and do the injections myself, or with the help of a doctor. In any case, I am going to leave here in the middle of next week, most likely the 25th. All of these doctors cost a lot of money, but I won't have to make use of their services so much after this, especially if I do my own injections, which is quite easy to do. Other than this, I am feeling very well.

No. 13 to his Mother

Hotel Logan, Denver, Colorado, 27 June 1891

Dear Mother

Just a few lines to tell you that I have gotten here safely. As I told you in my first letter, I had a free pass from Chicago. I have now gotten a free pass down to Durango, and then back to here again. I am going there to see the cliff-dwellers [sic]; on the way I'll visit Pike's Peak and other places. I have little or no money to buy minerals with. The 100 dollars I asked for will reach me in San Francisco, if they have been sent off by now. In the meantime, if I can get a free ticket to Portland on the Union Pacific, as I hope to, I'll get along just fine. The "Cliff-dwellers" which I mentioned lie about 45 English miles from the railroad station at Durango. Part of that distance must be made on horseback.

Denver, where I am today, is an important mining town in the foothills of the Rocky Mountains. To the East, one sees only endless plains, and to the West stands a long row of white, snow-capped mountain peaks.

Tell Father that I have now finished the final draft of my Mammoth Cave article, and that I'll send it soon, and that the Florida article was sent off the day before yesterday from Chicago. Right now, I must go visit the consul for Sweden and Norway. He is a very friendly man, and has been of great help to me. There is even a Swedish newspaper here in town, whose editor I was introduced to. Don't forget to send me copies of the newspapers containing my travel articles.

Greet everyone at home from Mother's devoted Gustaf

Write to me often, even if you don't receive letters from me. The next address: Yokohama Swedish Consulate

No. 14 to his Father

Hotel Logan, Denver, 30 June 1891

This evening, I shall travel down to Durango in southern Colorado, from whence I shall make a trip to Mancos Valley, where there are a number of cliff dwellings. From what I have heard, it seems to me that one ought to be able to obtain some crania and artifacts there. On the way back to Denver, I shall visit Pike's Peak. Luckily, I have gotten an open-ended train pass for this trip, but it still cost me 100 dollars. I am almost certain I'll be able to get a similar pass all the way to Portland, from whence I plan to travel down to San Francisco by steamer. I don't have a single cent left with which to buy minerals, but perhaps I can find some at Pike's Peak. It will be useless to look for samples in the mines, for everything in them has been picked up. My article on Mammoth Cave is only half finished. I'll complete it before I leave Durango. It doesn't seem as though it was such a good idea for me to bring along my mathematics texts; I haven't had a chance to even look at them since I left Europe. I wonder if Father has received my Florida articles and the boxes containing phosphate samples and bones. It would please me to find out how much you received for my articles. I am sending home a bundle of books which I do not need now, to my own address. It would be best to put them somewhere in my room until I return home.

The next letter will come to you from Durango.

Greet mother and the rest of the family from Father's devoted Gustaf

No. 15 to his Father

Mancos, Montezuma County, Colorado, 2 July 1891

I mentioned in my last letter that I intended to go to southwestern Colorado to see the so-called "Cliff dwellings" in Mancos Cañon. I travelled by train to Durango, and from there by horse and buggy to Mancos (5 Swedish miles). I found lodging there at the home of a farmer, Wetherill, who grazes his cattle in the area where the cliff houses are, and so is familiar with them. He himself is old now, and sits at home on the farm while his boys drive the cattle down into the valley. I decided to follow them down to a place where they had their camp, and from there to visit the ruins with one of them as a guide. It was my intention to spend about one week in Mancos Cañon. That week has now gone by, and I have decided to extend my stay to one or two months.

I want to first give a report of my first trip down to the ruins. On the first day, we rode 24 English miles down through the Mancos valley. On the following day, we rode up onto the "mesa," one of the eroded plateaus in the cañon, and then rode 10 miles along the same to Cliff Cañon, and on to Navajo Cañon, where there is a fine little spring. Water is otherwise difficult to find in this area. In the last-named cañon, we visited a smaller cliff house. It was reached from the top of the cañon wall. The descent was made easier by steps carved long ago by the builders of this house. The house lies completely within the sheer wall, the cliffs overhead forming a roof. The rooms were small, and the walls well preserved. From this cliff house, we rode back to a branch of Cliff Cañon, which we crossed by foot, leaving our horses on the level ground. On the other side lay a large group of cliff houses on a high cliff shelf. The place bears the name "Cliff Palace." If I can, I shall send a photographic view of it with this letter; it will be bound with a photograph of the Wetherills' latest collection.

From there we returned to the camp, arriving in the evening. On the following day, we rode down through Mancos Cañon to view some figures carved into the cliffs there. I have made some partial drawings of them. The day after that, I took two men with me and rode along the bottom of Cliff Cañon to a smaller cliff house which I decided to excavate. On the first night, we camped in the bottom of the cañon. The first afternoon, an entire day, and the following morning were spent in digging. The house consisted of 11 rooms; 2 circular, and the rest quadrangular or built to conform with the cliff wall. The roofs of the two circular rooms had collapsed, and

29

the walls were partially in ruins. In the first of these I found the majority of the items which are indicated below in a list. After concluding my excavations, I returned to Mancos, having spent a week camping out in the open air.

I mentioned in my previous letter that the only scientific expedition to examine these houses was Holmes and Jackson in 1874. They noted the existence of some ruins, and that was about all. One stone axe, a few pottery vessels, and some kernels of maize were all that they found. They made express notice of the absence of both people and animals (see my list 69, 115, 118). Probably one of the reasons why they did not excavate more thoroughly was that the Indians at that time were more hostile; now they are quite docile.

A few years ago, Wetherill's sons (cowboys, but with a surprising level of education) began digging in the ruins. During the first winter, they dug almost exclusively in "Cliff Palace," and put together an impressive collection of all types of household items, as well as a number of crania and several mummies, that is to say, human bodies preserved by drying, etc. The collection was sold to a museum for 3000 dollars.

Some time after that, they made excavations in several other cliff houses, and assembled yet a larger and more complete collection, which is now being offered for 8000 dollars. It consists of 5000 items. I include a sort of catalog of it here. Two workers who used to be under the employ of the Wetherills have since put together another important collection from excavations in another area. It has been taken eastward to be exhibited, and will possibly direct scientific attentions towards the region. As I have said, all of this work has been done by cowboys as a speculative enterprise. I am certain that in one or two months' time, I could assemble a beautiful collection which ought to be most valuable. It will cost me around 400 dollars, a sum which without a doubt can be regained many times over. I mentioned in my previous letter that it is difficult to work here in the summer, but according to the experience I have now gained, it will not at all be impossible.

I must remain in the good graces of the Wetherills, the only ones who know their way around this labyrinthine area. I want to ask you, Pappa, to send me a copy of *The Voyage of the Vega*, as well as the English synopsis of all of the journeys. Both the father and the sons are very interested in arctic research, and were quite familiar with your expeditions. This winter, they are planning to go down to Colorado Cañon, 250 miles away, to see the cliff houses there. It would not hurt if I followed along with them, and I am of a mind to do so. Even though such a trip would without a doubt also be covered by the sale of my collection, it would be best if a certain sum of money, around 600 dollars, could be procured for it. As far as the weather, this area is a natural sanatorium both in winter and summer. At present it is very warm in the daytime, and rather cool at night, and there is always sunshine. Only every now and then do we see a rain cloud, which obscures the sun for a moment while it discharges a small shower with a burst.

In order for you to get a proper idea about the Cliff dwellings, Pappa, I ask you to read the chapter on the Cliff dwellers in Nadailloc, *L' Amérique préhistorique* [Jean Francois, Marquis de Nadaillac, L' Amérique Préhistorique, Paris (1883)-Ed.] and compare it with the catalog enclosed here. I am very curious to hear your opinion on the matter. It would be good if Father could send answer by telegram yes or no as to whether I should stay on longer here. I am too far away to communicate by correspondence before I undertake something new. If you feel that this work is of importance, please send my camera. It consists of the following parts 1) camera 2) tripod 3) objective lens 4) cassette for photographic plates 5) shutter and 6) dark cloth, as well as my barometer, if that has not already been sent off. There is no good series of photographs from these remarkable ruins in existence. My letters during the next weeks will be very sporadic, for I will be entirely cut off from civilization. My address for letters as well as telegrams is Mancos, Montezuma County, Colorado, U.S.A.

31

No. 16 to his Father

Mancos Valley, 3 July 1891

At present, I am in southern Colorado, 30 [American] miles from the nearest railroad, and 6500 feet above sea level. I am staying with a farmer and cattle rancher named Mr. Wetherill. It is very beautiful up here in the mountains; the only problem is that it's rather warm during the day. I am getting along just fine with the cowboys here, who strangely enough seem to have just as much education, if not more, than many businessmen from the higher classes in this country.

I have come here to see the cliff dwellings in the Mancos Valley. In Denver, I had the chance to find out just how much is known about them. As far as I can tell, the only scientific expedition which has examined them was the Jackson and Holmes party in 1874. The former was a photographer, and the latter was a geologist. The result of the expedition seems to have been only a small number of photographs and a rather incomplete knowledge of the appearance and extent of these remarkable buildings. Since then, the matter has been handled only by cowboys and dilettantes. The former have made some excavations, and have brought to light a small collection which now belongs to some corporation in Denver, and more recently, a large, excellent collection which is up for sale for 8,000 dollars (a high price, since 2,000 dollars would probably be enough for an expedition which could recover a very complete collection). This collection consists of pottery vessels, general household items, mummies, skeletons, etc.; items which as far as I know have not been described in writing.

Another equally as important collection (2500 items) has been put together by a miner who is interested in these matters, and his colleague, another dilettante, over the course of several winters, in an area 100 miles west of Mancos, in southern Utah. It now belongs to the church in Durango, a little city in southwestern Colorado. Naturally, none of these excavations have been organized in any scientific way. There are still a number of cañons which have never been explored, and many of the others have not been examined in a complete manner. It is now summer, and is so hot that one could scarcely think of making an excavation.

At any rate, it will be interesting for me to see these remarkable things. I will be spending one week down in Mancos Cañon, 30 miles from here, where the Wetherills' cowboys have a campsite. This area would be an excellent research field for Martin or some other ethnologist. One of the parties which has gone out looking for "cliff dwellers' relics" brought along a photographer. I shall try to get copies of his photographs; they could be of interest to some museum.

In a week, I shall return to civilization and post offices once again, and shall report to you on what I have seen.

Many greetings from Pappa's devoted son Gustaf

No. 17 to his Mother

Mancos, Montezuma County, Colorado, 15 July 1891

Yesterday I received a packet of letters which had been forwarded to me from San Francisco. Included among the letters were two from Mamma, the first I've had in a long time. As Mother has probably already heard, I am going to stay on here in the area of Mancos for a while longer. Mancos is a small town in southwestern Colorado. For now, I am staying with a farmer named Wetherill, high up in the mountains.

When my next advance of money arrives here from San Francisco (probably tomorrow or the day after tomorrow), I will set out on horseback for Navajo Cañon, 38 miles from here. Yesterday, I sent two men ahead of me with equipment. The region is completely wild, and lies within an Indian reservation. The Ute Indians are now of a peaceful disposition. I will be spending a longer period of time out at my field camp, busy with the task of digging for antiquities in the "Cliff Houses." The house which I am planning to excavate is among the largest, about 480 feet long. I will not have many opportunities to send you letters, except for the occasions when I shall ship home loads of artifacts.

I now own two horses; one is a small, wild black pony which I myself ride, and the other is large and slow, which I use as a pack horse. Here everyone knows how to ride, and the only way to get around in these wild, bleak mountain areas, cut up here and there by cañons, is on horseback.

[Letter continued on-Ed.] 17th July

The advance arrived here yesterday from San Francisco, so I shall be leaving again tomorrow. I am also sending off an article about Mammoth Cave in Kentucky today.

Greet everyone at home, and write soon to this address: Mancos, Montezuma County, Colorado, U.S.A.

Mother's own devoted Gustaf

No. 18 to Karl, a cousin

Mancos, Montezuma County, Colorado,
18 July 1891

Dear Ka-cousin

Your lengthy epistle gladdened me greatly, and it makes me happy that you are in the best of health. It might amuse you to hear the peculiar way in which Fate has taken me of late, such that I will now be living in "the Wild West" for months. It is also Fate which has transformed me into an archaeologist, an owner of two horses, etc., etc. I came to Durango, a city in southwest Colorado, with the intention of making a little excursion to view some peculiar and interesting ruins, "the Cliff houses."

I travelled 5 Swedish miles from Durango by horse and buggy to Mancos, where I lodged at the house of a farmer who grazes his cattle in the desolate area where these memories of a long-since disappeared people lie. He, or more correctly, his five full-grown sons (genuine cowboys) know the area well, and had even undertaken excavations under their own initiative, with most remarkable results. Even so, their discoveries do not seem to have awakened the interest of any scientists. I decided to make a week-long excursion to the ruins, and to dig a little bit as an experiment. The ruins lie 5 Swedish miles south of Mancos. The Mancos River cuts through a great plateau, forming a deep valley, or cañon, which connects an extremely complicated system of side-cañons, these being narrow valleys with high, vertical sides, with a dry river bed at the bottom. In the middle of these steep walls the ruins lie like eagles' nests, often barely accessible. On the first day, we rode 25 English miles down to a camp which the

34

cowboys had in the Mancos Valley. The following two days, we visited ruins which were reachable only after much strenuous riding. On the fourth day, we rode up to a cliff house which has not yet been excavated, and took our camping gear with us. For nearly three days, I searched around for antiquities with the help of two men, and even found a thing or two.

Camp life has always been a pleasure for me, and we were quite comfortable down in the bottom of the cañon. There was, however, one circumstance which put a bitterness into our days. It was during the summer heat wave, and almost everything was dried out. After much trouble, we were successful in finding a small hole containing some water, which tasted quite awful. But, oh, thou spring of misery! We did not notice our mistake until it was too late. It was a spring of the most horrible, falsified water, and if we had swallowed half a stein full of turpentine, or had drunk 20 liters of Hungarian bitter water, we would have had a hard time feeling any worse. Luckily, we had concluded our excavations, and could head immediately for our main camp. I had hardly recovered when I almost ate myself to death on some sort of poisonous candies. At any rate, despite all of the difficulties, I intend to stay here one or two months and dig, so that someday you may find yourself sitting, writing a catalog of broken pots, large and small, and of mummies, cadavers, and crania of the cliff dwellers.

If you would like to have something nice made by the Indians, I might be able to get it for you. The Navajos weave excellent and beautiful red and patterned blankets, 20 dollars for a good one. I have gotten myself a pair of very beautiful saddle bags of buckskin, embroidered with small beads in a very beautiful and original pattern. About 100,000 beads were used in the embroidery, which must have kept one of their squaws busy for 1/2 year or more. I might be able to dig up some small, ever-so-ancient pot for you, if luck smiles upon me. In any case, I hope that you will remember me again soon with another epistle.

Your devoted cousin, Gustaf

address Mancos Montezuma County, Colorado, U.S.A.

This is a reproduction of page 3 of letter **No. 19 to his Father** written by Gustaf Nordenskiöld on July 29, 1891. At that time he was working in several cliff ruins on Wetherill Mesa.
(Photo courtesy of the Center for History of Science, Royal Swedish Academy of Science, Stockholm.)

No. 19 to his Father

Strater House, Durango, Colorado, 29 July 1891

I have come in to Durango for a day to pick up my money. I collected the second advance [of money] a few days ago. I left my camp in Navajo Cañon early yesterday and rode 45 miles into Mancos. Today I rode the 30 mile distance in to Durango, so I am feeling a little stiff in the legs. I have spent about a week out at the camp, drawing, photographing, and excavating.

Among the finds made in the excavations, I want to mention as the most remarkable a grave. Although not complete, the skeleton is well-preserved. It lay with the legs drawn up to the chin and the back facing outward, buried under a projecting portion of the cliff. We were able to see the remains of a low wall which had been built outside of this area. Near the head lay a large bowl, and within this was another very small one with a handle. The skull, which is in perfect condition, has been artificially flattened in the back. Among the other finds, I want to mention a necklace of seashells with holes bored through them for stringing, some beautiful stone tools, a piece of cotton fabric with an interwoven pattern, etc.

Already, I would like to begin writing about these, if I can find time. Early tomorrow morning after I've taken care of my errands here, I'll begin riding back to my camp, which should take about 3 days, since I must bring along two packhorses loaded with provisions. I am most curious to hear what Father has to say about my excursion to Navajo Cañon and my archaeological research. The economic side of the matter ought to be of little concern, or at least, it would be, if the collections were to be sold here in America, but which, of course, I will not consider doing. Neither the Smithsonian Institution nor any museum in Europe has any collection from the cliff ruins of Colorado.

The region is also interesting from a geological perspective, with its complex system of cañons. The actual distance between my camp and Mancos is considerably shorter than the ride on horseback, but to travel in straight line it would be necessary to pass through perhaps 10 cañons, which on horseback would be impossible, and on foot would be difficult and extremely strenuous. The rivers which created these cañons have dried up, but here and there one can find water. The theory which has been put forth as a surety, that the precipitation was more favorable

37

during the time when the ruins were inhabited, is completely without grounds. It is much more likely that the climactic conditions have been the same as they are now. However, it is certain that the cliff-builders were deeply involved in war. The house wherein we are now working consists of a large lower level, and an upper level. In a cross-section, they look like this:

[Drawing of cross-section presented on page 36 -Ed.]

The upper level is extremely inaccessible, and we haven't been able to get up there as of yet. The inhabitants must somehow have made use of the walls in climbing up. This upper level has served as a fortress— for the walls are full of shooting-holes [for bow and arrow]. In order to get down from the top of the mesa to this ruin, we had to make quite a lengthy detour. It is interesting to see how the inhabitants have made their climbing easier by hewing steps into the cliffs, which even we now make use of. Up on the mesa, there are remains of dams, which have served to collect rainwater. These finds indicate that the climate has not changed to any noticeable degree, for if the rainfall here had been greater, there would have been enough water without building the dams.

The whole mesa is strewn with bits of pottery, in some places so thickly that one cannot help but trample upon them when walking. This shows that an extremely numerous people must have lived in this region, where today one meets only an occasional Ute Indian. There are also building ruins on the mesa, but they are poorly preserved. The same is true in the bottoms of the cañons.

But now to return to the cliff-ruins, which because of their protected location are quite well preserved, despite their less-than-solid method of construction. The most remarkable rooms in the ruins are the so-called estufas, which in the pueblos of the present-day Indians is said to be the keeping-place of the holy fire. These must also have served as some sort of general-purpose room, since they are often full of general household items. The floor plan is as follows

a) is a round hole which is filled with ashes, and has obviously served as the fireplace.

c) is a narrow passageway which at point

d) turns straight upward. It is not sooty, and is thus not a chimney. Possibly, although this would have been quite uncomfortable, it was the entrance to the room. This is something which I cannot yet ascertain.

b) is a low wall, which in such case might have served to protect those entering from the fire.

About seven feet from the floor is the roof, which in most cases has collapsed. The roofs are built of *Juniperus* logs (here called "cedar") with smaller sticks laid across them, and a layer of some sort of mortar over the whole. At a height of about 3 feet above the floor, there are 6 niches separated from one another by 6 pillars. The former are about 5 - 6 feet wide. The interior of the estufa is covered with a yellow plaster. One can make out several sooty layers, one over the other. The smoke must have been let out through a hole in the roof, although a good portion of it seems to have stayed in the room. In each ruin, about half of the total number of rooms are estufas. However, there are also many small ruins which have only 1 to 3 rooms and no estufa. Of these ruins, some are completely inaccessible, given the means available to us out in the field. In some places, portions of the cliff have collapsed and buried some of the ruins, or have destroyed the means of access to them. The weather has carved out projecting shelves, which one must often follow a long way before finding a way up or down. In many places, one can see several different building methods, which ought to indicate that the walls have several times been destroyed and then rebuilt. The same observation may be made of different parts of a ruin, the houses seeming thus to have been built gradually and with long intermissions.

It would be very interesting for me to visit the Zuñi and Moqui, two tribes of present-day pueblo-dwelling Indians. They do not live so far away from this area. It might possibly be wise to publish on these things I've written about. It will be a while before you receive another letter from me, for I intend to stay at my camp for at least 14 days before returning to civilization. I do not have much to say about my health; it is excellent. Greet everyone there at home.

From your devoted Gustaf

Please write to me often at
Mancos, Montezuma County, Colorado

No. 20 to his Mother

Mancos, Montezuma County Colorado, U.S.A., 31 July 1891

Dear Mother

Thank you for the letter which was sent to San Francisco. You ask me to tell more about my travels. I have already sent in two long newspaper travelogues, and the third is just on its way. It is about the Cliff-dwellings in S.W. Colorado, and ought to be more interesting than the others, since they dealt with things already known to you.

If it will amuse you, Mother, I'll tell a little bit about what it looks like where I am now—not Mancos, which is a civilized place, but Navajo Cañon, 7 Swedish miles from that outpost of civilization. Try to imagine a forest of low pine trees and a type of tall juniper bush, called "cedars" here. I do not know if they are the same sort which grow in Lebanon, which are said to be very large. In any case, our cedars here are hardly any taller than the large juniper bushes at our house in Dalbyö.The ground here is sandy and half bare.

One can see a large tarp made of sailcloth stretched out between two trees; this is our bedroom, that is, mine and my foreman's. Ten steps away there is a dirtier tarp; under this one, two Mexicans sleep. One of them speaks some English, and he is a great rascal. I sent him to Mancos the other day to buy provisions and some canned goods which would have brought a welcome change to our monotonous diet of flour. Upon his return, he told a story of how one of the packhorses had bolted and lost some of its burden (5 of the tastiest canned items were missing). He and his friend had devoured 4 cans of preserved fruit which I had ordered for my own lofty self. A short while after, I rode into town along the same route myself, and had the satisfaction of seeing a number of opened cans with the most beautiful labels, strewn along the side of the trail. Furthermore, Joe (for that is the scoundrel's name) had received one dollar as his wages, and with this had bought whiskey, returning to camp drunk. I am only glad that he did not leave the area with all three of my horses. But this is enough about Joe; let us return to the campsite.

If one clambers under my roof, one will see a real bed, that is, a cot, made of split juniper trunks. We have beds like this to protect ourselves from a most unpleasant sort of animal, which I will tell more about very soon. Beside the cots, one can see a great pile of saddles, saddle blankets, spurs, bits, etc. Two steps outside my "room" there is a table, a real table. It is somewhat à la Robinson Crusoe, but it is a table nonetheless. Over the same, there is a tarp, dirty and soiled. Under the table, there is a raised box for keeping provisions out of reach of the above-mentioned unpleasant animal. A little bit away from the table (which could be called the dining room) lies the kitchen, even less impressive than the dining room, for it is only a few burned-up logs, except for cooking time, when a cheerful campfire burns there. Below the kitchen, about 20 to 30 steps away, lies our spring, which is the reason why we have set up camp 1/4 Swedish mile away from our workplace.

A spring is something rarely seen in this area. Our spring has in its favor that it does not contain a sort of American bitter-water, as do other springs. This bitter-water tastes worse than the strongest turpentine when it is used in tea, coffee, oatmeal, etc. I had a stomach ache for a whole week after undergoing such a "cure" at the first ruin I excavated, and during that time ate little more than 3 pieces of bread and 4 glasses of milk. In the meantime, I have recovered and have gotten fat. From the same spring (that is, the one in our camp), we water horses, who also graze nearby with a rope fettering their front feet. As Mother can see, I am now just as great a horsekeeper as Mother and Father together. However, my experiences as such have not been the best, as one of my horses ran away a few days ago, and another was lame, while the drunken Mexican had succeeded in breaking the third. I'll have to rent horses, in exactly the same way as when we travel to Gnesta. The runaway has come back, but the lame one is still lame, and "Old Rigg" still has a bad back.

We begin our day at about 6 o'clock. I have the privilege of stretching out a bit longer, while Joe gets the horses, and John, the foreman (who gets 3 dollars a day, that is more than 10 crowns, or more than a full professor's wages in the Old World), cooks breakfast. Breakfast usually consists of bread, baked here in a kettle, fried pork, oatmeal, coffee, tomatoes, and sometimes rice and cooked apples. We cannot get fresh meat; it keeps for only 2 or 3 days in the heat. At the signal of "Breakfast ready!" we gather around the dirty table, which is cleared of everything palatable in an incredibly short time. The dishes are washed, whereupon the horses are saddled up, the canteens are filled, and we head off along the narrow trail to a place on the mesa above the ruin where we are working. We take off the saddles, and fetter the horses' front legs. (I am running out of paper! This is being written on the backside of one of Pappa's letters. Letters from Mother never seem to have any blank backside.) Then we climb the long roundabout way down to the ruin. There we dig, draw, take photographs, and label, etc., until the sun stands in the middle of the sky. At that time we have our lunch break, which consists of nothing more than a can of corned beef and a piece of bread, for we cannot bring much with us. After this we work until the sun begins to sink in the West, and the shadows on the cañon walls become long. Then it's up into the saddle again, to ride home to camp. Soon the campfire is flaring up, and the teakettle and baking oven are placed on the flames, and dinner, with approximately the same menu as breakfast is served up, and possibly a little more hastily.

Sometimes after dinner, we set snares for the above-mentioned unpleasant animals, always with negative results. And so we go to bed; I in my sleeping bag (I am introducing this unequalled contrivance to the area!). Just as I am ready to fall asleep, I hear a suspicious rustling very close by. I look to the left, and see a large, fluffy tail. Another person might clap their hands, or try other means of violence to get rid of the uninvited guest, but woe be unto he who does so. The long tail belongs to a so-called "skunk," an animal which at the first sign of danger "makes a big stink," or, to say it in good Swedish, spreads the most infernal odor. People known for their truthfulness claim that a skunk can be smelled 6 miles away, something which I nonetheless have reason to doubt. In any case, it is certain that if we let him release his stink, we will have to "pull our freight" and head for a new place. This is the reason why I quickly put away my revolver, and with slow movements carefully encourage the pest to go away. But this is not the only one; around our camp there are about a dozen "skunks." It is our store of pork that they want to get at; I fear that soon we may have to give them all of it to get rid of them.

(I am still short of paper! I am writing this part of the letter on the lower half of a bill for the same pork which the skunks want to eat up.) Despite all of the skunks, we fall asleep quite soon, awakening the following morning to begin the same routine.

Next letter in two weeks!
Many greetings from Mamma's devoted Gustaf

No. 21 to his Father

Mancos, 14 August 1891

I am once again in from my camp, to stock up on provisions.

I have been on a ten day trip on horseback through the southern portions of the Mancos Cañon system, and have seen much of interest, but only a few new ruins. During this time, three [of my] men have continued the excavation work.

Among the finds which ought to be mentioned are several crania, some beautiful stone tools, a bowl of stone, and etc. Today I am sending a small box home, and will soon be sending more. The box contains a number of small items found at different times. Next time, I shall send some crania and skeletons.

It is my intention, if Father does not have any feelings against it, to stay here until November, and travel home at Christmastime, postponing the rest of my travels until some other time. Continually living outside and the healthy life out in the field are beginning to make me brown and fat, so that the main goal of my trip has more or less been achieved. Besides, I shall soon be speaking fluent English. I hope to come home with a beautiful collection and a rich harvest of observations. I am sending a bundle of some photographs of myself as a cowboy.

Greet Mother and the others at home from
Father's devoted Gustaf

P.S.
I will probably be spending a long time out in the wilds this time once again, and may make a trip to see the Blue Mountains, 70 miles from here.

My economic affairs are organized such that 175 pounds have been transferred from my credit sum, and deposited in the First National Bank of Durango, and which I am now using to meet my expenses.

Couldn't 8,000 dollars be gotten from some rich man in order to buy Wetherill's collection? It is one of the two or three [good collections] in existence, and is certainly the most complete. It will soon be impossible to obtain any collections of these artifacts, for it looks as though the authorities intend within the near future to intervene in any such purchases.

No. 22 to his Mother

Mancos, Montezuma County, Colorado, 15 August 1891

I am impatiently awaiting letters from home. It is now one month and 4 days since I wrote home and gave you my address.

I have spent the last period of time exploring some as of yet unknown cañons. For 12 days, we (I and one of Wetherill's boys) rode up cañons and down cañons, trying to follow unclear cattle paths, or searching for some narrow, stony path between the cliffs, made by the Indians. Sometimes we must even make our own trail through tight undergrowth. Towards the evening, we must always search for a watering hole. Rainwater gathers in some of the depressions in the sandstone cliffs; this water is usually old, yellowish and full of insects. Such holes are few and far between. One evening, we searched until nightfall, and continued to look in the weak moonlight, but found not a drop of water. We spread out our horse blankets and wrapped up in our quilts. Despite hunger and thirst, we soon fell asleep. The following morning, as soon as the stars began to fade, we continued the hunt for precious water. About 100 paces from our camp, we found a large pothole filled with rainwater. Off with the horses' saddles, and a substantial super-breakfast [sic] was prepared, with coffee, tea, rice, and oatmeal, as well as bread. First, however, we had to think about watering the horses.

The water lay in a small cañon with steep, although not high, walls. There was no way in which to get the horses to it. We looked over our cooking utensils. A coffee pot and frying pan were all we had. The former was too narrow; this left only the frying pan. A rope was tied to an empty tin can, and with this instrument, water was hauled up and poured into the frying pan. Each of our three horses drank about 50 frying pans full, so we had a lot of work to do before their thirst was slaked.

This was the only time when we did not have water; otherwise, we lived quite well and had plenty to eat. One evening we were even so lucky as to discover the best spring in the entire area, with clear, cold water. Above this grew the most beautiful grass for the horses. We returned three nights in a row to this lovely spot.

This next time, I shall probably be out in the field for about a month; it is possible, however, that I will have the chance to send off a few letters. On the other hand, if no letters should come, there should be no cause for alarm.

Many greetings from Mother's devoted Gustaf

No. 23 to his Father

At the campsite in Navajo Cañon, 18 August 1891

I am just now sending a load by packhorse to Cortez and then on to Durango and Stockholm. If the boxes should be unpacked before my return, please be sure that the skeletons from the different sacks are not mixed together. Another box has been sent previous to this.

Hastily, Gustaf

No. 24 to his Father

At the campsite in Navajo Cañon, 23 August 1891

Thank you for your letter, Father, which I finally received yesterday. I have recently fallen into some difficulties with the authorities, but everything has been cleared up now. One of the area's two largest merchants became dissatisfied with me, since I bought all of my supplies from the other. He sent some sort of report to interested authorities, stating that a foreigner was busy destroying some of the most beautiful ruins. The result of this was a public notice in the Mancos post office, to approximately the following effect :

Nobody is allowed in this reservation for the purpose of procuring Indian (!) relics from Aztec (?) ruins... No foreigner is allowed on the Indian land without permission... fine 1000 dollars.

"1000 dollars" had a negative effect upon me. I rode in haste to the nearest military station, where I obtained without difficulty a pass which allowed me to be on the reservation, but which also

45

had the inconvenient addendum that "this pass do not [sic] include any right of making excavations in the ruins."

Through an influential acquaintance in Durango who is a good friend of the Indian agent, I received the message that no one would hinder me in my excavations as long as no ruins were destroyed. In the meantime, I have sent home the items I have already obtained, just to be sure. My plans now are as follows : until the end of September, I shall stay here in the Mancos area, occupied mainly with studying the cliff ruins. By that time, I should have a rather beautiful collection from there. After that I will go directly to the Grand Cañon in Colorado [sic] and from there by horseback through Arizona, New Mexico, Texas, and possibly a bit of old Mexico, to the East Coast, and from there take the shortest route home, whence I ought to arrive at around Christmastime. I may need some more money, but will be arriving home with a profit of 3000 or 4000 crowns, perhaps more, if I can get my collections out of here. A good camera will probably cost me about 100 dollars. My camera there at home, with all its equipment, has cost over 500 crowns. My collections here are increasing all the time. Beautiful stone tools, more crania, woven items, etc. I am presently employing 4 men for a total of 7 dollars per day in wages. To feed them and myself costs about $1.50 a day. I own 5 horses, representing a total value of 150 dollars. One has run away, and another is poorly saddle trained. The climate and the lifestyle here has the most healthful effect upon me.

If I tell people that I am travelling for the sake of my health, they laugh at me. I am beginning to get fat (I have had to let out my underwear by 4 inches). How much did you get for my newspaper articles? I'll send more of them in the form of letters to Mamma. If any of my collections are unpacked, please see to it that bones from the different skeletons are not mixed up; they have been packed each in a separate sack. Has the phosphate report been printed anywhere? I am impatient to get more letters from home. My address is still the same, at least until the middle of September.

Many greetings. Pappa's devoted Gustaf.

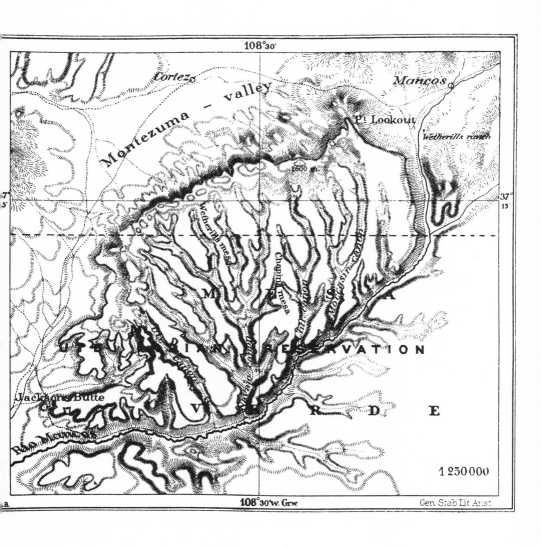

Map of the Mesa Verde
from Gustaf Nordenskiöld's *The Cliff Dwellers of the Mesa Verde-*
Southwestern Colorado: Their Pottery and Implements. (1892).

No. 25 to his Father

Mancos, 29 August 1891

Three copies of *The Voyage of the Vega* have arrived. I have sent off only a small box with samples from my collections. All the rest is still here, and I intend to send everything at once, since that is cheaper. At this time I am breaking up camp, and will be going southward to the Moki Indian reservation there, and from there a few hundred miles further to the Grand Cañon. From there, I may go through old Mexico to the Atlantic Ocean, and then take a steamship directly home.

Under somewhat odd conditions, I have employed two of Wetherill's "boys" (cowboys) as escorts and assistants for collecting during this trip. I pay only for their food and their trip home, and they will leave their pack horses with me. Thus this trip will be relatively inexpensive, and ought to yield interesting geological results as well as some rich entomological and botanical collections, which might possibly pay for the entire cost. The journey will take about 2 months. The climate in the mountain regions, and camp life have the best influence upon my health, as I have previously mentioned. I have been negotiating with a firm in Denver to buy a camera. It will be quite expensive (150 dollars), but the photographs will surely bring that sum. I will also need the 600 dollars which you named, Father. We should be able to recover them on [the sale of] the collections. The collections I already have ought to be worth at least that much. Please send the money, immediately, if possible, to this address Mancos, Montezuma County, Colorado, U.S.A. It would be best that the money be transferred by registered letter to an American bank.

The volcanoes in Mexico should be extremely interesting.

The method of travel which I have become accustomed to here in the West offers the best opportunity for observing these regions. With my camera, I intend to take the best series of photographs in existence of the Mancos region and of the cliff dwellings. In these ways, I hope to transform my tourist trip into a rather productive scholarly journey. I'll be home in the beginning of '92.

Many greetings Pappa's devoted Gustaf

No. 26 to his Mother

Mancos, 29 August 1891

Dear Mother

Thank you for the letter you sent from Finland. I am once again in Mancos to take care of a number of errands. I have very little to relate from camp. The excavations have continued, and many items have been found. I am on good terms with the Wetherills. It is in their interest to keep me here, for I rent and buy horses from them, etc. Several hundred dollars have already wandered from my pockets to theirs. I also have one of their boys in my employ, and he gets the tidy sum of 3 dollars (over 10 crowns) per day in wages. I have sent off a small crate of artifacts. It should be unpacked very carefully. Just now, I do not have anything to relate to the newspapers, but in a month I shall travel southward through wild and remarkable areas, and will again have quite a lot to tell about. It would be fun to know how much you are receiving for my travelogues, and if my phosphate report has been published anywhere. Please send me everything that comes out. Either today or tomorrow, I shall send you two photographic views of the Rocky mountains and one of Niagara Falls to hang on a wall somewhere. Greet everyone at home from

Mamma's devoted Gustaf

No. 27 to "B . B."

Mancos, 30 August 1891

Dear B.B.

I must hurry to answer your much-welcomed letter of unknown date, and let you know of my thankfulness for it. As you can see, I am still here in Mancos, digging and rooting around among the antiquities; pots, axes of stone, knives, etc.; everything imaginable, including the most surprisingly fossilized 1000 year old pieces of s- - -! [sic]

9 September
Have not finished yet, but have again come in to Mancos for a few days. Have made some excellent finds: the mummy of a dried

baby, many pots, etc. I myself rode into town with a gigantic, extremely fragile pot— tied around my neck! I intend to make a long journey through Arizona and other wilderness areas, perhaps even old Mexico, but will remain here for another month, digging in the cliff-ruins. I am extremely busy. Sometime I will send you a few views of this place. I have bought a camera for 150 dollars, double the size of the last one I had. I intend to take 200 pictures. If you should want to come and visit me, I'll give you one of my pots and a horse.

Write soon, or to say it more correctly, at once, if your epistle is to reach me in time.

Your friend,
G. Nordenskiöld
Mancos, Montezuma County, Colorado

No. 28 to his Father

Mancos, 31 August 1891

Enclosed here is an essay on the ruins in the Mancos area. It was thrown together in a hurry (my time was limited). The title is "The Cliff Ruins in Southwestern Colorado." It ought to be good for an article in *Stockholms Dagblad* [a newspaper], and it also contains a few things suitable for a scientific journal (such as *Ymer*); especially since the region I have written about is so little known. Early tomorrow morning, I'll go with one man and a packhorse to explore some cañons which have heretofore been visited only by Ute Indians. We will possibly, or even surely find ruins there. My next letter will come in about 9 days.
Greet everyone.

Hastily, Gustaf

No. 29 to his Father

Mancos, 9 September 1891

Thank you for your letter of the 19th of August, Pappa. I was in Durango yesterday and sent off 9 packages (7 crates and 2 barrels) of Cliff dwelling collections. I addressed them to the Swedish Consulate in New York, and have written to the consul that he should send them to the Mineralogical Department of the National Museum, which is going to pay for the freight charges. I tried in vain to get insurance on these items but it cannot be applied to so-called "Aztec relics." The value of the collections ought to be as high as 1500 dollars, if they could be appraised. They have cost about 1000 dollars. When I am done here in about a month, my collections will be worth a total of about 10,000 Swedish crowns, if they were to be sold here in America. They will, however, have cost me only half of that, provided that I continue to find as many artifacts as I have been able to thus far. As I mentioned, the most recent work here has been rather successful. The collection now includes a mummy. Have also recently found what is perhaps the most beautiful pottery vessel yet excavated here, a large, spherical pot about 18 inches high and decorated with patterns. I am sending a list of the crates and their contents; this should be paid attention to, if the items are unpacked before I arrive home.

Regarding the geology of this region, I shall now mention what I know. Layers of basalt or other "staircase" form outcroppings are not to be found. The plateaus are built up of a massive layer of sandstone which lies almost horizontal, so that they slant at about $10-20°$ longitudinally towards the cañons. Sometimes the sandstone is interrupted by beds of slate. In some places, the sandstone itself contains fossilized shellfish, and occasionally, leaves, although poorly preserved. Layers of coal also occur in several places. In one place, a massive eruption has thrust up through the sandstone, forming an entire mountain. In another location, I have seen yet another eruption. I have heard that gas jets can be found in a cañon not far from here, and intend to explore that area at my first convenience. Also, I have heard rumors of a gigantic skeleton, with shoulder blades 7 feet long, in the San Juan riverbed. It would probably be difficult to find, but I shall try. I am in a hurry, and am soon going out to my camp. Camera is on order, 100 dollars, with photographic plates. Intend to take 200 views of the ruins.

Greet everyone at home. Pappa's devoted Gustaf

51

No. 30 to his Father

Mancos, 16 September 1891

Dear Father

I already have an impressive collection of relics, and will be sending off a shipment of 8 crates to the Swedish Consulate in New York tomorrow (the 17th of this month). It is getting to be time to leave Mancos. An ignorant newspaper article containing expressions such as "vandalism," "robbery," and "must be stopped at once" appeared soon after I had made my first shipment, which is why I prefer to get the rest of my collection to safety as soon as possible.

Among the latest finds there are a mummy, several new graves with pots and bowls, and a large black pot of a sort which is often found in small bits, but seldom whole. (I do not know if this is true, but it is claimed that a similar pot was sold to the Smithsonian Institution for 2500 dollars.)

When I have gotten my photographs finished, I intend to go southwards to the Moki Indian reservation. This should be around the 5th of October. In the meantime, the excavations continue with 5 men, and I am still hoping for further valuable additions to my collection. The little crate which was sent by "express" must have arrived by now. It contains an especially beautiful stone knife and a stone axe with handle. If it would not be too expensive, it would be good that Pappa could inform me by telegraph of the mailing date for the 600 dollars which I wrote about earlier. In regards to the unpacking of my crates it would be best to let me unpack them when I arrive home. It is important that the contents of each crate are kept separate. It is possible that some labels were forgotten when the boxes were so hastily packed. Furthermore, some boxes contain portions of a skeleton which I will be able to organize when I arrive home only if everything is in the same condition as when I packed it. I have not received any letters in a long time. I hope to hear something from home today, for I am just now riding into town to collect my mail.

Pappa's devoted Gustaf

No. 31 to his Father

TELEGRAM

The Royal Swedish Telegraph Service

Sent from Durango, Colorado, America, 17 September 1891

Nordenskiöld, Stockholm, Sweden
"Much trouble some expense no danger
Gustaf"

No. 32 to his Father

Mancos, 19 September 1891

Yesterday, I sent you the following telegram:

Nordenskiöld, Stockholm, Sweden *"Cable to New York 600 dollars with instructions to wire to First National Bank in Durango through Chemical National Bank in New York. Gustaf"*

The reason that I need money in such a hurry is that people here have begun to oppose my excavation and work in a way that makes it desirable for me to soon leave this area. In the meantime, I shall remain here no matter what until the beginning of October. 9 of my crates will soon have arrived in New York. I have 8 more in Durango which may be confiscated. Americans would rather that cowboys, miners, etc., dig amongst their antiquities, than foreigners. I am now going on a photographic trip for about a week, after which Pappa will once again hear from me.

Greet everyone at home. Letters from you are getting very scarce.

Pappa's own devoted Gustaf

No. 33 to his Father

Durango, Colorado, 27 September 1891

I suppose that the telegram has already brought a report about my misadventures. Even when this letter arrives in Sweden to tell you that I have been successful in clearing up the difficulties through the help of friends, I can imagine that a complete report will be of interest I have already told you about a posted announcement, aimed at myself, in the Mancos post office, from a Mr. Bartholomew, the local Indian agent.

Shortly thereafter, I received a letter from a friend of mine, Mr. Ritter at the U.S. Land Office, stating that if no ruins were destroyed, I would be left alone. Besides this, I had further reason to not worry about posters in the Mancos post office as my camp was located not on the Ute Indian reservation, but several miles north of it. In any case, because of the notice, I hurried to Fort Lewis and obtained a pass. Specifically, I wanted some freedom in the event that my explorations should take me over the borders of the Indian reservation. However, the fact remained that I had been within the Ute Indian area earlier. It was because of this that it was found prudent to arrest me, since no one whom I spoke with had ever even heard of the commanding officer at Fort Lewis, who had issued my pass. This was, however, only their excuse.

The real reason behind it all was that about one month earlier, I had packed and sent off 9 crates (600 pounds) to the Swedish Consulate in New York. A schoolteacher publicized this fact through an ignorant article in the *Durango Herald.* When I saw this article, I hurried to pack up the rest of my collections (8 boxes), and tried to see Justice Newcomb. The man had disappeared, and I fell asleep in his office. At Newcomb's office I had to pay a fine of 1000 dollars, or rather, a gentleman by the name of Mr. Wilson paid that fee for my freedom. In the meantime, Mr. Ritter sent a written report of the whole affair to his good friend, the U.S. Attorney General, encouraging him to issue orders that the proceedings be closed. I further sent my lawyer, Mr. Wilson, to Denver to attempt to sway Colorado's attorney general. During this time, I went back to Mancos for the purpose of taking pictures with my newly arrived camera. This entire spectacle was set in motion by a few farmers who see the ruins and the treasures to be found in them as a good source of income for the future. They have even gotten a few Indians to complain to the Indian agent. What they have to complain about is difficult to know, since we have not seen a single Indian in our vicinity during the entire time there.

The general mood among the leading men is one of indignation over this affair. But the matter has gone much further than this; it has gone all the way to Washington. The Swedish legation there has telegraphed and asked me about the situation. Furthermore, the "acting Secretary of State" has telegraphed to the mayor of Durango to make inquiries. The latter answered with a telegram giving details and asking that the proceedings be halted. My collections are safe; some in a cellar in Durango, and the rest in Denver. In a few days it will be decided whether or not the proceedings will continue. In the former case, I will be burdened with many difficulties, but can hardly be seized or deported. In any case, I shall remain in Mancos for 2 more weeks to finish my photographic work. I have received the 600 dollars. Also got a cable from Erland which I do not fully understand.

My judge, Mr. Newcomb, is a passionate spiritualist, and has given me a book which one of the old Moki Indian kings has written through him as a medium. I met him on the street one day and thanked him again for the interesting book, which resulted in my being invited in to his office, where he gave me a half hour long lecture, read from a manuscript, about the earliest settlements in Scandinavia according to spiritualist revelations. It was worse than being put on trial ten times!

More tomorrow or the day after. Greet everyone. Pappa's devoted Gustaf

No. 34 to his Father

Durango, Colorado, 30 September 1891

Things are beginning to look brighter, and, at any moment, orders to drop my case are expected. I'll telegraph either tomorrow or the day after once everything is in order. In the meantime, all this has cost me 200 - 300 dollars, and in order for me to be able to travel home to Stockholm, I must ask you to send 300 dollars more to the Swedish Consulate in Denver. I have had to pay terribly high freight charges. I will probably send the collections by express in order to avoid more quibbling, and to get them away from the claws of the Yankees. This will cost about 200 dollars, but the collections are now worth about 3000 dollars, at least, here in this country. I will also be sending a number of saleable items, especially from the Navajo Indians, and perhaps from the Moquis. If this letter does not arrive in time for the money to be sent off by the 22nd of October, it would be best to send them around the 1st of November to the First National Bank of Durango, via New York, as was done with the 600 dollars which I previously received.

My travel costs have been as follows:

	Swedish Crowns
Letter of credit, 5000 marks	4,500 crowns
Letter of credit, 4000 francs	2,800 crowns
Letter of credit, 175 pounds	3,150 crowns
2 advances, total 200 dollars	730 crowns
1 advance of 600 dollars	2,190 crowns
Last advance I received,300 dollars	1,095 crowns

Total	14,465 crowns

The money which you gave me at the start of my trip ought to be regained through the sale of my collections, which also (along with my newspaper articles) ought to pay for a good part of the rest, too. As mementos, I'll have an excellent camera and a large number of photographs.

I'll be home by Christmastime.
Pappa's devoted Gustaf

No. 35 to his Father

Durango, 3 October 1891

This evening a U.S. prosecuting attorney will be arriving for my own special pleasure. It is said to be certain that the case will be dropped; I will telegraph the results to you this evening. From your letters of the 10th and 13th of Sept., respectively, I understand that you wish me to continue my travels westward, Pappa. Naturally, I have nothing against this idea. It is only the economic side of the matter which has scared me.

As a result of your letters I have made the following plans: as soon as I am finished here in the Mancos area I shall make a two-month trip to the cañon region of northern Arizona. (Travelling to Pike's Peak to look for samples now during the snowstorm season is hardly sensible.) During my expedition to Arizona, I will have rich opportunities for geological studies. I have procured the help of two cowboys, as well as a young man from Durango. This entire two-month trip will probably cost about 200 dollars. I will have gained good material for some nice newspaper articles, and some fine geological collections (freight charges will be uncomfortably high!), as well as some ethnographic collections which might help to pay for the costs of the trip.

Upon my return to Mancos from this expedition, I'll travel to San Francisco (at around New Year's) and continue to travel around like that, to return home in May. As far as the economic aspects of things, my situation is thus: I have (as well as the 300 dollars which I requested by letter a few days ago) received 500 Swedish crowns. In order to travel all the way around the world, I will need about 5000 crowns more. All of this is on the condition that the legal proceedings here come out happily for me. If my collections should be confiscated (which is hardly likely), I shall return home by the most direct route possible.

I have kept lists and notes on all of my finds, and want to publish a larger ethnographic or archaeological work. If you approve of the above-mentioned plans, and if you receive a telegram to the effect that my case has been dropped, please send an advance of 275 pounds [sic] (like the previous advance) to Mancos, Montezuma County, Colorado as soon as possible; preferably before the 15th of November or before the 25th at the latest. That way the money will reach me when I return to Mancos from the Arizona trip. I am not sure that people in Sweden will see as much value in my cliff dwelling collections as they do here. The mummies (2 of them) and the skeletons (about 6, with several more crania) ought at least to be seen as valuable, as well as the stone tools (about 100 examples) and the pottery vessels (about 40). One must take into consideration that these items are from a vanished people, and that similar things are hardly to be found in any European museum. The entire collection now consists of about 600 items.

My address until the 25th of November is the same as it has been. I'll write again tomorrow, once my fate has been decided.

Many greetings Pappa's devoted Gustaf

The Swedish consul has been energetically working on my behalf in this legal matter.

P.S. 5 October: Case dismissed, everything all right. I am thus without any hindrances to the continuation of my travels, and hope that my collections arrive safely. It might be a good idea to send them to the exposition in Madrid, but in such case, someone would have to travel there to receive them and put them in order. Perhaps I can arrange things so that I myself am there at that time. Please write back about this, and tell me the dates for the exposition.

No. 36 to his Father

Strater House, Durango, Colorado,
7 October 1891

I am now free from any further inconveniences resulting from my arrest, but whether or not I can save the first half of my collection is still uncertain. The whole matter is too long for me to give a complete report on, but it has taken a lot of time and money. If I can only get my collections home, all of this will mean little. That the case has had such a happy ending is largely due to the efforts of a Mr. Ritter of Durango, who has many friends among the leading men in Washington. If I will now be able to get my collections to Stockholm, this will also be due to his help, so I stand in great debt to him. Could you, Father, send me some beautiful item from Sweden which I could give him as a present (perhaps your atlas)? His wife is an enthusiastic collector of antiquities, and would be delighted to get one or several Swedish stone axheads, or something similar. Best to send these things as soon as possible to my usual address. I'll thus receive them around Christmastime, when I have returned to Mancos from my trip southward.

Please telegraph me as soon as my crates arrive in Stockholm, for I am very concerned about them. Greet everyone there at home

from Pappa's devoted Gustaf

No. 37 to his Father

Strater House, Durango, Colorado, 21 October 1891

I have been out in the cañons for 14 days on a photographic trip, and have taken about 100 pictures. Upon my return I received two letters from you, Father, which (in contrast to your previous letters) tell me that you want me to come directly home. I myself want to come home as soon as possible, and finish writing my report on Spitsbergen, as well as my intended works on the Mancos ruins.

All of the ridiculous quibbling and arresting is now completely over, and I have permission to ship out as many relics as I want. However, the whole fiasco, which began without any real reason, has cost much time and money. Just now, my attorney came to me and plundered me of 100 dollars, and I shall soon be without money again; a dollar is worth almost exactly one crown at home, sometimes even less. To get a shave costs 15 cents, about 50 Swedish öre. A glass of beer also costs about the equivalent 50 öre. Coins smaller than a nickel (about 15 öre) are not to be seen at all. I won't be able to come home unless you send me the 400 dollars which you named in your last letter. (That is, $400 plus the cable fees). If any cable transmissions of money have been sent off after this one, I haven't reckoned with them.

The freight charges for my entire collection are now almost 250 dollars, plus the 100 dollars for the entire legal matter, for a total of over 325 dollars, or 1300 Swedish crowns. In a week, I'll be going to Arizona, to return after 2 months, and be home in January. I have written to the consul in New York, and instructed him to bill the freight charges, New York to Stockholm, to the Mineralogical Department of the National Museum. The first shipment, which has been on its way to New York for a month now, contains only the first half of the collection. The rest of the items are still in Durango, since I do not have money to ship them with. It would be best to send the money directly to Mancos, to some American bank, and preferably in an unregistered letter.

Letters from me will probably be quite scarce while I am out in the wilds. Hope to gain yet more material for some good newspaper articles. I got a terribly unpleasant surprise when my attorney came and asked for 100 dollars more from me. Altogether, he has gotten 250 dollars, and has done a lot less for me than my friends have. These idiotic legal proceedings in their entirety have cost me over 400 dollars, and have been of no benefit to anyone. Even without the intervention of the Swedish foreign minister and other lofty individuals, the matter could not have ended other than with my vindication, although it would have taken longer, perhaps half a year. It seems now as though the officials do not want to grant me a pass for the purpose of travelling through the Navajo Indian reservation; a new "China" in the most free country in the world.

I am beginning to get bored with all of this, and feel a little homesick. However, for the sake of completing my study in a thorough way, it is absolutely necessary that I visit the Moki Indians.

Greet Mother; I shall write again just as soon as I have something other to report than quarrels, arrest, and interrogation. Please greet Erland and Anna as well.

from Pappa's devoted Gustaf

No. 38 to his Father

Strater House, Durango, Colorado, 22 October 1891

In my letter yesterday, I forgot to mention that I have sent home a small box by mail. In the box is a bottle containing the remains of snow which was said to have fallen with a red coloration. A complete report on the occurrence has been promised to me. Pappa's devoted

Gustaf

P.S. To be observed when my collections from the Cliff dwellers are unpacked:
No. 1 Large crate containing a mummy and a skeleton, half mummified, etc.
No. 2 Small keg containing stone tools, etc.
No. 3 Large crate containing pottery and other fragile items. Should be unpacked carefully; in the large pot in the center, there is a skull.
No. 4 Barrel containing a large, beautiful, but extremely fragile & thin pot. Should be handled carefully.
No. 5 Diverse skeletons and bones.
No. 6 Stone Items.
No. 7 Miscellaneous.
No. 8 Pottery, etc. Careful!
No. 9 A complete skeleton.

G. N.

No. 39 to his Mother

Mancos, 23 October 1891

Dear Mother

During the last few weeks, I have been a poor correspondent, but that was because I had so much else to bother with. Now that things are once again in order and my collections are on their way to Sweden, I am beginning to feel more at ease. I have recently been on a photographic trip around Mancos Cañon, and have brought back more than 100 beautiful views, which I am now busy developing.

Pappa has sent me a letter which had come to Sweden from America, along with a photograph. He wrote that he "hoped it did not contain any secrets." It was from a young (and very beautiful) American woman, Miss Wight, whose acquaintance I had made during the voyage over the Atlantic. Just today I received an announcement of her marriage. She was an artist and was very spoiled. She had been in Rome, had bleached her hair, and had made a collection of about 50 dresses, all of which had to be shown off on board the ship, such that each one was worn for only 1/2 or 1/3 of a day.

In about a week, I leave for my Arizona trip. I have asked the Department of the Interior for a pass for travel through a Navajo Indian reservation, but it looks as though this will be denied to me. Now I will have to make a detour through Utah, north of the Grand Cañon, a very wild and miserable half-desert region. Altogether, we are six persons: myself, my two cowboys, a young man from Durango, Mr. Tetar, as well as two other youths.

My collections will soon be on their way home. Some of them may even be in New York, where the U.S. government has finally discarded its plans for confiscation.

I shall have more to write about once I begin travelling, but since the post offices are few and far between my letters will not come so often. Thank you for your letters of the 29th and of the 6th of October. Greet everyone from

Mother's devoted Gustaf

No. 40 to Karl, a cousin

Mancos, 23 October 1891

Dear Ka!

I am still here in Mancos despite all of the trouble. My collections will travel ever so calmly home to Sweden, and everything is once again in the best of order. Your letter gladdened me greatly, and I had just been thinking that I needed my Ka-cousin's help, now if ever. I have just completed a 10-day "photo trip" with my camera, and have taken over 100 views, which I am now splashing about with and developing, with the most fantastic results. I am sending the plates directly home, and do not have time to make any co-kapies, I mean, Ka-copies. I am hoping for your gracious help at some time in the future. The format will be approximately double my old one. As soon as I am finished with my photographing, I will leave this unthankful area, and ride southwards through Arizona for a two month trip, and then home in January. I long to be able to put my pottery in order and finish my book on the Spitsbergen trip, as well as some other worthy undertakings. I'm tired of wandering around the world with nothing to do.

I have a beautifully patterned Navajo blanket worth about 50 crowns, which you can buy from me, if you wish. I'll also bring you a piece of pottery as a present.

In the area where I shall be travelling there are said to be a lot of bears, panthers, wildcats, antelope, deer, mountain goats, etc. Once we kept a bonfire blazing all night because we had seen panther tracks very close to camp. Another time, I woke up when I heard a rustling in the bushes, but it was only a "big stinker" (a skunk) or a "little mouse." On my trip to Arizona, I will be accompanied by a party of 5 men, so that my scalp remains relatively secure. For safety's sake, I have gotten my hair cut quite short, so that the value of my scalp will be more problematic.

I have also made quite an interesting collection of newspaper clippings, wherein Mr. Nordinjskod or Kortinskid or worse is accused of "carrying away the ruins from the Mancos Cañon," etc., and saying that "he ought to be lynched."

You'll get to see all this and more when I come home. Scalped or unscalped, I remain your devoted cousin Gustaf, and I hope for more letters from you soon at this address.

No. 41 to his Father

Mancos, 1 November 1891

Yesterday I returned from my last trip down into Mancos Cañon. I had been busy completing my photographic work on "the Cliffhouses." I now have a series of 138 photographs, partly in the same format as my Spitsbergen pictures, and partly in a format twice that size (18 x 24 cm.) I also visited an area which is thus far unknown, where there are jets of hot natural gases. I was taken there by one of Wetherill's boys. If one follows Mancos Cañon for about 30 miles, one will come to the mouth of Grass Cañon, which runs almost directly in a north-south direction.

Along Mancos Cañon, there are three sites where eruptions protrude directly upward through the completely horizontal sandstone. In Grass Cañon, about three miles from where it meets Mancos Cañon, there is a similar eruption which may be traced on both walls of the cañon. Grass Cañon has a different character than the rest of the side cañons. Its walls are less steep, and are more broken up. 6 miles from the mouth of the cañon, the trail winds its way from the bottom of the cañon up to the mesa. It then runs along the peninsula formed between the main cañon and a side cañon. At its outermost point, this peninsula is lower than the rest of the plateau, and is made up of slate with a lively red color, and of an appearance which one does not see elsewhere. This slate is obviously metamorphosized through some process, perhaps in conjunction with the above-mentioned gas jets. In other areas, these hard red slates are replaced by a loose, gray slate, under which lie beds of coal without any recognizable fossils. Under the red slates, there is a layer of snow-white stone (perhaps talc?). After following the trail further, a short ride took us to an area full of ditches and holes, from which steam arose. It is believable that this steam was mixed with other gases (since it had an obvious smell, like petroleum or burned asphalt). However, it does not kill the surrounding vegetation, and moss grows especially well in the moist areas around the holes, as close as the heat will allow. Some of these rifts are several feet wide, and so deep that the bottoms are lost in darkness.

We continued to follow the mesa in a southerly direction for about 3 miles, and came to an open area, very much like the previous one. However, at first sight, it became clear that the gas here was of a much more dangerous character. The ground here was bare, and the vegetation was dead or very sickly. I walked up to one hole and leaned over it to examine it. The gases were expelled with loud noises, like that of an underground fire. The smell was faint and the gas was completely dry (there was no trace of condensation on my eyeglasses). The gas has transformed the sand all around the rifts to a whitish material with a very sour taste (alum). Within some of the holes themselves, we could see shiny white crystals. It was not without difficulty (since the gases are hot) that we succeeded in taking samples of this material. It has the same sharply sour taste as the white compound in the sand. Finally, I made an experiment with an insect, a grasshopper, which I was able to catch after much chasing. When exposed to the effects of the gas, it fell asleep after 1 to 3 minutes, but woke up again after 10 to 15 minutes. The gas is probably carbon dioxide, and its source must be the underlying coal beds, which are probably in the process of some sort of chemical transformation.

On the 3rd or 4th of November, I will be leaving Mancos to take my trip to the Grand Cañon, and to visit the Moki Indians. I will have the company of a man named Al Wetherill, who has visited the area west of Mancos before. I had expected more companions, but they have cancelled.

The second half of my collection probably left Durango several days ago by express, and will thus probably arrive in Stockholm before the first shipment, which went out by "freight." Freight shipment led to much annoyance, and the people involved in shipping felt that they had the right to examine the goods, etc., which is why I preferred express shipment, which was only a little more expensive. Altogether, 18 boxes (or more correctly, 15 crates and 3 barrels) at a total of 1400 pounds have been sent out. On both shipments, some of the shipping charges will have to be paid in Stockholm.

I may possibly be home for Christmas, otherwise in January. As far as my personal economy goes, I need the 400 dollars which I wrote about earlier; with that money, I will be able to get home. So that I may know in good time that the money has been sent, and when I can expect to receive it, I ask that you send a telegraph to Mancos, Montezuma County, Colo. Telegraph to me the date of the cabling, to which address they have been sent, and the sum.

During my time in camp in Mancos Cañon, only the following fossils have been found:

1. 2 or 3 sharks' teeth in sandstone.
2. 3 or 4 types of dichotomous leaves at one location, the sandstone somewhat fragmented, but well preserved, and some bits of mussel shells.

Layers of basalt do not exist, only small outcroppings protruding straight up through the sandstone.

In conjunction with these eruptive outcroppings, one also finds Icelandic spar.

Many greetings from Pappa's devoted Gustaf

Articles from the Journal
Ymer
the
Swedish Journal of
Anthropology
and
Geography

Translated by Daniel M. Olson

THE BALCONY-HOUSE

On some remarkable ruins in Southwestern Colorado

By G. Nordenskiöld

(Translated from *Ymer*, the annual journal of Svenska Sällskapet för Antropologi och Geografi, 1892, pp. 3-13.)

Our earliest knowledge of the areas north of present-day Mexico date from the era when the Spaniards, having conquered the Aztecs, and driven by the desire for gold and new lands, began to make their way further north. Under the leadership of Alvar Nuñez Cabeza de Vaca, the few last surviving adventurers of an expedition to the northern coast of the Gulf of Mexico had forced their way directly across present-day northern Mexico, from the Atlantic to the Pacific coast. During their journey, they heard tales of large, well-peopled cities located to the north of their route. They brought these rumors back to Mexico, and filled their countrymen with enthusiasm for further explorations north-ward. A plan to send forth a conquering army was met with widespread public support, and volunteers signed up in droves. The governor of Nueva Galicia (the Spanish colony in western Mexico) Francisco Vasquez de Coronado sent a number of smaller scouting expeditions to these areas, most of which we know little about. Only one of them is of any great interest.

Followed by a fellow monk and a Negro, the Franciscan monk Marcos de Niza made a journey to the north from Culiacan in Nueva Galicia. The Negro Estevanico, who was sent ahead as a scout, was the first man [*sic*] to cross the border between present-day Arizona and Mexico. From the natives they met along the way, the Spaniards received confirmation of rumors they had heard concerning the existence of large cities to the north. They were told that region was inhabited by a people who built houses of stone, wove cloth of cotton, and wore turquoise as jewelry. Estevanico, driven by eagerness to make a discovery, ranged on ahead of the rest of the expedition. Eventually they neared the city of Cibola, which they had heard spoken of. The main body of the group, led by Niza, had only a day's march left when they were met by several men from Estevanico's scouting party, who related that the Negro had been slain by the inhabitants of Cibola. Niza made a hasty retreat and returned to Nueva Galicia. Upon his return home, he described for Governor Coronado in such colorful terms what he had learned about the extraordinary riches which would be found in the cities to the north that Coronado himself equipped a larger expeditionary force in order to conquer these areas for his country.

This expedition departed early in 1540. When after much effort and tribulation the storied city of Cibola was finally reached, and had been taken with only weak resistance by the inhabitants, the conquerors found themselves bitterly disappointed. Instead of a great city, they found only a miserable little village. Of the great riches of which Niza had spoken, nothing was to be seen. The inhabitants did indeed wear turquoises, but great troves of this precious stones were not to be found.

The belief that greater riches might be found further northward did, however, drive the Spaniards on to continue their exploration. Through reports on military conquests made in different directions from Cibola, we have today quite a complete knowledge about the geographical distribution of these city-dwelling (or so-called "pueblo" dwelling) Indian tribes in Arizona and New Mexico. The Spaniards' descriptions also provide us with knowledge about these Indians' way of life during this time. If one excludes those changes which have come about through the introduction of iron, it can be said that these tribes lived at that time completely in the same way that they do now. They subsisted mainly upon the cultivation of maize, wove cloth of cotton, and kept turkeys as livestock; and they built houses of stone, often several (up to 7) stories high, in terrace form. In these traits they were quite separate from the nomadic tribes which inhabited outlying areas. The geographical distribution of the Pueblo Indians was approximately the same then as now, if one excludes from consideration the facts that some villages have been abandoned, and that the population has now been quite reduced.

As well as inhabited pueblos, the Spaniards also came across ruins. Great numbers of such ruins, usually in a very advanced degree of decay, are still in our day, to be found throughout an area covering all of Arizona and New Mexico as well as parts of Utah and Colorado. The ruins in the southwestern portion of the last-named state have been the object of my examinations.

Before I begin my description of the ruins found in this area, a short description of the local geography will be useful. Colorado is, as is well known, very much an alpine region. The highest mountain tops rise up to heights as high as 15,000 feet. However, in the southern part of the state, the landscape takes on an entirely different form: in place of the high mountain tops and rugged alpine terrain, one is met with a monotonous, half-desert environ, with desolate, widely-spread out plateaus which rise in terrace form above one another. These plateaus are usually carved by many deep, narrow furrows caused by erosion, commonly called "cañons," to use the Spanish name, which has been adopted by the Americans. Far down in the southwestern corner of Colorado, in the outreaches of civilization, where the pioneer's log cabin stands beside the Ute Indians' recently abandoned "wickyup," a large plateau called "Mesa Verde" rises above the landscape. The name, which dates back to the time of the Spaniards, refers to the fact that this mesa, in contrast to those further south, is tightly clothed in a forest of small cedars and pinion (*Juniperus occidentalis* and *Pinus cembroides*), two hardy species of conifer which are able to withstand the area's searing summer heat. The climate is extremely dry, and rain falls but seldom, except during the rainy week which occurs in the autumn, when heavy showers followed by thunder and lightning fall upon the land, followed by short interceses of quiet.

Flowing through Mesa Verde in a southwestern direction is the Rio Mancos, which, after taking leave of the pioneer settlements of the same name, runs through a narrow cañon, which is formed as the valley walls close in upon themselves. From the level of the riverbed up to a height of about 400 feet, the valley walls slant steeply. Above this height, they run completely vertical up to the top. Here and there in these vertical cliffs, located in small, grotto-like shelves which would seem better places for eagles' nests than human dwellings, a sharp eye is able to discover a few half-fallen stone walls. In their color, these walls do not distinguish themselves at all from the surrounding sandstone cliffs. Most of the cliff dwellings found in the Rio Mancos' cañon are quite humble. Many of them are so well hidden, and so similar in appearance to the cliffs around them, that only those who are very familiar with the area, and who have had opportunity to examine every little niche in these cliffs will be

71

able to find them. In the course of 20 miles, no less than 50 such cliff dwellings are to be met with.

Running off from either side, Mancos Cañon has widespread systems of side cañons, which form veritable labyrinths. These side cañons are to a great extent much like the main cañon, and like the latter also contain numerous cliff dwellings. Many of them are even larger than the ruins in Mancos' cañon. Within the entire Mesa Verde area, that is, within the entire Mancos cañon system, there ought to be around 500 cliff dwellings. Besides these, there are at the bottom of the cañons, and at the tops of the cliffs a number of other ruins. These, due to their less well-protected location, are in an advanced state of decay, such that it is impossible to distinguish individual walls among the ruined heaps.

Ten years ago, only a very few of these ruins were known to exist in this area, all of them located in the Mancos Cañon proper, their discovery being the result of a research trip made by some geologists employed by the American government. Then in the beginning of the decade following 1880, a farmer from the town of Mancos began to drive his cattle out upon Mesa Verde. During the hikes and explorations which resulted from this, one ruin after the other was discovered, each one successively more grandiose than the last, located in the depths of remarkable, high-vaulted caves. Excavations were made in these ruins with promising results, and it was the stories about these excavations which convinced me to lengthen a tourist visit of a few days into a several-month long stay for the purpose of scientific examinations.

My first trip out from the town of Mancos was to the two largest cliff dwellings, "Cliff Palace" and "Spruce Tree House." With our provisions loaded upon packhorses, we made our way about 24 miles through the Rio Mancos Cañon on the first day. That night, we slept on the banks of the river, and broke camp early the next morning. We followed the river a few miles further, and thereafter took a winding Indian trail up the slopes to the top of the plateau or "mesa." We made our way in a northerly direction along this steppe, an extremely monotonous ride along sandy soil and through a low forest, where each tree was exactly like the next, and where the branches were grown so close that one had to bend forward to the horse's neck, or throw oneself off to the side of the saddle to avoid having clothing or skin torn to shreds. Those who were at the head of the party fared the worst; those who came after got through at less cost.

Suddenly the forest thins, and in a moment, the most grand and peculiar sight spreads itself before the eyes of the rider. We stand at the edge of a precipice. In the cañon wall directly facing us on the other side, in the depths of a high-vaulted grotto, a confusion of towers and walls rise up out of gravel piles. This is "Cliff Palace," the largest of all the known cliff dwellings, discovered by R. Wetherill and C. Mason in 1888. The name given this ruin is well-deserved. The cave in which the buildings stand has a depth into the cliff of 125 feet. The number of rooms on the first level is 125. The upper floors are not usually extant, and in the few cases where they are, the floor joists are always missing. I will not here allow myself to go into any closer description of this proud edifice, with its numerous rooms, towers, and thick walls. In its method of construction, it does not differ from other ruins, which I will attempt to depict later on. During this first trip, one other ruin was visited, namely "Spruce Tree House," the next-largest after Cliff Palace.

After returning from this, my first visit, I began at once to make preparations to undertake excavations. We outfitted ourselves with the necessary provisions, and set out, three men, for a ruin high up in Cliff cañon, which is a branch of Mancos Cañon to the northwest side. We made camp in the dried-out riverbed in the bottom of the cañon. From there, a strenuous climb took us up to our intended work area. We had first to creep upward through a tight covering of brambles on a steep slope for about 300 feet. Near the end, completely vertical cliffs took over, requiring us to claw our way upwards with our hands. Once at the level of the ruin, we were able to walk upon level ground. From the narrow shelf upon which the buildings are raised, and where we now stand, it would surely have been easy to turn back an attack, even one by a quite numerous enemy. It could only have been the necessity of having to be constantly on guard against an enemy more superior in numbers which would have made the "Cliff dwellers" take refuge in such naturally fortified places.

Let us now take the ruin itself into closer consideration. The walls are still very well preserved; this is of course entirely due to the well-protected location, for the roof of the grotto juts out quite a ways over the shelf, and so completely protects the whole ruin. This is the case with all cliff dwellings. If any buildings have at some point lain outside the protection of the cliff "roof," their walls are almost always destroyed; the mortar has been washed away, and the stones have fallen down.

Among the gravel piles and half-fallen walls of the ruin wherein we now stand, we are able to discern 11 rooms. Of these, two circular rooms in the approximate middle of the ruin are of greatest interest. Both are built upon exactly the same plan. The inner diameter of the circle is 12 - 15 feet, and the thick walls are completely cylindrical inwardly, built up of carefully hewn sandstone. Towards the top, about 3 feet from the ground, the wall is divided into six niches, more than a foot deep in the wall itself, and divided by equally as many six-sided pillars. One of these six niches is recessed deeper into the wall than the others, and underneath the same runs a passageway, level with the floor. The passageway is several feet wide, and is 5 feet in height at first, thereafter going straight out and up into the open air. Inside the "estufa" itself, in front of the passageway, stands a low wall. In front of this wall in the middle of the floor is a round pit which obviously served as a fireplace, since it is still full of white ashes. To find ashes in such considerable amounts shows the falsity of the opinion put forth by another party that these cliff dwellings were only occasional places of refuge during times of crisis. A number of other points also counter this supposition; for example, in the plaster on the walls of the rooms we find many different layers, which have one after the other become begrimed with soot and then been covered over with new plaster.

These above-mentioned round rooms distinguish themselves in their form and plan from the other parts of the ruin. Such circular rooms, all built upon exactly the same plan as the above, are found in all cliff dwellings, with the exception of the smallest ones, which contain but one or two rooms. They correspond in all likelihood with the rooms which are to be seen in the dwellings of the Pueblo Indians, called by the Spaniards "estufa." This term indicates a room of a specific plan, usually sunken halfway into the ground, serving as a gathering place for religious and political meetings. The secret ceremonies which are connected with the annually-occurring ritual dances take place in these rooms. The estufa is also occupied by the men when they busy themselves with weaving and other handwork, these tasks being undertaken by the men of the Pueblo tribes. In the hearth in the center of the estufa, the eternal fire burns, or more

74

correctly, glows— for this fire is never allowed to burn with a flame. The entrance to [these Pueblo estufas] was through a hole in the roof, since there were no doors in the walls. This is still the case with the estufas of the Moki Indians of today. There can be no doubt that the circular rooms in the ruin which I have just described, and in the cliff dwellings in general, have served the same purpose. The estufas found in the cliff dwellings differ from these partly through their shape, since the Moki estufas are rectangular, and partly through their unique entrance arrangement with the passage or tunnel leading out to the open, as was described above.

The other rooms in the ruin which I have described above are of rather small dimensions (6 - 8 feet in either direction). Their shape is usually rectangular, but is also often influenced by the location and height of the surrounding cliffs. These walls are built up of roughly-hewn sandstone pieces; usually about one foot thick. The rooms lie seemingly without any planning along the shelf. A somewhat higher shelf also has several rooms built upon it. The stones are laid together with mortar, the joints having been given added strength by the insertion of stone shards. The doorways, which also serve as windows, are so small that one must always crawl in through them. They could be closed by means of a flat slab of stone, which could then be bolted with a wooden beam thrust through sockets located on either side of the doorway for this purpose. In this way, the cliff dwellers were not allowed any great amounts of fresh air or light. Some of the rooms farthest back against the cliff wall are so small and low, that if one is successful in squeezing into them, one will be unable to turn around, and would be forced to crawl out backwards in the same position. Some of the ruins in these cliffs consist of only one or several such holes, often located so high up in the steepest wall that one searches in vain for a means of access. How might the cliff dwellers have done, since they had not only to carry themselves up to these points, but also building materials, tools, etc.?

We began our work in this ruin by digging out the most well-preserved of the two circular rooms, which was filled to a depth of 2 to 3 feet with gravel, collapsed ceiling beams, dust, and large amounts of cactus thorns which had been dragged in by rats. The fruits of our labor were a number of artifacts, mostly unremarkable, but still of interest, since they provide us with a glimpse into the way of life of the former inhabitants. I shall at this point give an account of the most important finds:

Maize kernels in considerable amounts. This cereal was cultivated, as is still done by the Pueblo Indians today. Judging from the great amounts of it found, seems to have been the most important foodstuff of the inhabitants.

Beans of a brown variety. This crop is also still cultivated by the Pueblo Indians.

Bits of the shells and seeds of pumpkins. The top of a large shell had been cut off, and the bottom then sealed with pitch, to form a drinking vessel.

Cotton fabric, well and evenly woven. Cloth with an inwoven pattern was discovered in another ruin.

Sandals braided from yucca fibers. Yucca is a long-leafed Liliac [sic] which grows in great quantities on the plateau. Its sturdy fibers were the chief material for the making of rope and string, as well as for some weaving purposes. Yucca was found in the form of harvested leaves and already-loosened fibers, as well as finished string and the fabric woven from such string. This is a peculiar sort of cloth made by tightly interweaving turkey feathers, from which the shafts had been cut off, in amongst the yucca fibers, to form a net. The dead were wrapped in such feather fabric, before being interred. Coronado mentions that such a fabric was also made by the Pueblo Indians. Today the method of making it seems to have been forgotten.

Clay pots in any state of completeness were very few in number. They were of the simplest type, dark brown in color, and without ornamentation. However, shards of other pottery types were found, and we later had opportunity to dig up well-preserved examples of these types in other ruins. The most common type is white, with black ornamentation consisting merely of straight lines in simple, but tasteful patterns. Another variety is black, with dense, horizontal grooves, and sometimes, although seldom, with simple patterns in relief. A third variety, the most seldom found, is red with black and white ornamentation. Of the red pots, I have never found a single example in its entirety, only enough shards in sufficient enough number so that the shape and color of the vessel could be reconstructed. Small fragments of

76

all of these different types of pottery are found everywhere in great amounts, in the vicinity of the ruins as well as up on the plateau, especially on the grave mounds located there.

Tools of stone, bone, or wood. Of metals, not a trace is to be found. The stone axheads are of a number of different types. Besides the axes, finds of knives, arrowheads, hammers, etc. were also made. The finds of bone tools consisted partly of awls (made of turkey bones), and partly of a type of knife with a rounded edge presumably of deer bone). Turkey bones are especially common, and several conditions, such as finds of large amounts of turkey excrement within the ruins, show that these birds were kept as livestock, as was the case with the Pueblo Indians during the time of Coronado's visit, and still is with the Moki Indians today.

A bow and *arrows.*

A firebow of the same appearance as those which are still sometimes used by the Navajo Indians.

Combs made of small bundles of finely-bound twigs. Such combs are still used by the Moki Indians.

Rings made of yucca leaves to be placed under round-bottomed pots or for carrying loads on the head.

A large number of other objects, altogether over 100, were found in the ruin. Due to the completely moisture-free atmosphere of the site, all objects were in an excellent state of preservation. Almost all of the finds were made in the one round room. In the others, only a few objects of any interest were found. We worked for only a few days in this ruin, moving our activity thereafter to another area rich in large, noteworthy ruins.

From the town of Cortez, 15 miles west of Mancos in Montezuma Valley, a trail leads up to the foot of Mesa Verde, which rises 2000 feet over the plains. Leading up to the top of the plateau itself is an almost indiscernible riding-path, known only to the Indians and a few white men. Let us suppose that we have made the strenuous ascent, and now find ourselves up on the mesa. Our path takes us along its northern edge, over some not especially deep cañons. After having made many roundabout turns in order to pass these, we now go off to the right along a part of the plateau cut off from the rest by many cañons, and to which I have given the name Wetherill's Mesa. This portion of the plateau has a length of about 10 miles, and a breadth which varies from a few dozen paces to several miles. In the walls of the cañons on either side of this mesa lie numerous ruins of considerable beauty. "Long House" has a length of over 400 feet, and more than 60 different rooms. I cannot here go into closer description of all of these ruins, each one of which has some special point of interest. Let us, however, look more closely at one of them.

"Step House" is a ruin on the eastern wall of Wetherill's Mesa. The name derives from the fact that a stairway of large sandstone blocks leads down from the top of the mesa to the vaulted cave where the ruins are located. The buildings themselves take up only the westernmost part of the cave. Otherwise, the area under the cave roof is flat and completely free from any walls. This area is covered in some places to a depth of up to 6 feet with refuse, mostly turkey excrement mixed with remains of maize and diverse other types of scrap. In this refuse pile, we discovered a large number of graves, most of them located in a row far in under the cave roof. In general, the graves had been prepared in the following manner: a grave of suitable depth was dug in this rather firm soil, wherein the body was placed in a rolled-up position, with the knees drawn up to the chin. Prior to interment, the bodies were first wrapped in the above-described feathered fabric, and then further bound with yucca string, thus forming a complete bundle. After the body had been laid in the grave, a roof of crosswise logs was built over the same, which was in turn covered with a flat stone or a mat of withies bound with string. Over the whole was spread a thin layer of earth. Sometimes the dead were lain directly in the earth, wrapped in a mat of withies. One of the bodies which was found in this burial area had been completely transformed into a mummy by the extreme dryness of the air. Of the other bodies, the skeletons were well preserved. The skulls always showed signs of having been severely flattened [during life] by artificial means. With the adult dead were always buried one or more clay pots, and sometimes maize, or a basket of maize flour. Most of the clay pots which we were able to come across were grave finds.

It is very seldom that we find as many graves together as were found at Step House. The dead were usually laid to rest in some out-of-the-way crevice of the cliffs, in tiny burrow-like caves under the edges of the cliffs, or in some similar place. On several occasions, we even found graves within the masonry walls of the buildings themselves. It happened while we were working in the ruin called Long House, that the wall of the room next to that in which we were working collapsed, revealing an entire skeleton. Once, in a ruin located in Johnson Cañon, the Wetherill brothers found not less than five bodies, partially lying over one another, sealed into a room. A number of clay pots, arrows complete with stone points, a bow, and etc. had been buried with the dead.

But now to come back to Step House, we found, besides burial objects a number of items which had clearly been buried on purpose, perhaps to hide them from an approaching enemy. Among these, several large, beautifully formed clay urns deserve to be mentioned. Despite the comparatively short amount of time which we spent in excavating Step House, we found many more artifacts of greater value there than we had been able to find during a month of digging in other ruins. In addition, all of the objects were extremely well-preserved, and in most places, not a trace of moisture, which might have damaged the more delicate goods, such as textiles, etc., seemed to have penetrated the earth.

Some miles east of Wetherill's Mesa and separated from the same by several cañons, lies another portion of plateau with vertical walls. In the caves in these cliffs are the largest ruins in the entire area, and certainly in all of North America. One of them, "Cliff Palace," contains 125 rooms in its ground floor. The half-fallen walls in many places show us that several floors have existed in the past. In association with, and lying in close vicinity to the same are two other large ruins, "Balcony House" and "Spruce Tree House." At many points in the last-named ruin, the floors are preserved in their original condition. The door openings to these rooms are very small, and the rooms themselves quite dark. A rectangular hole in the corner of the ceiling gave access to the upper floor. No ladder seems to have been used, several stones projecting from the wall providing instead the necessary foothold.

About 20 of the 125 rooms in Cliff Palace are "estufas." These follow exactly the same plan described previously here, with the exception of only two, which are rectangular with rounded corners. The peculiar passageway leading out to the open air does, however, show that these rooms also served the same purpose as the others. It is possible that these two estufas show the transition from the circular to the completely rectangular form which occurs among the Moquis. In their method of construction, these ruins do not differ from the description given above. In particular, Balcony House, which lies on an especially inaccessible shelf in Cliff Cañon, is especially well-constructed. The building stones have been carefully hewn, so that the outer walls are completely smooth. In the same ruin, there is a very well-preserved balcony formed by projecting roof beams. This balcony provided communication with the upper rooms, the doors of which all open upon the outer wall.

A detailed description of all of these ruins would be too lengthy for publication in this journal. However, before I bring this short article to a close, I would like to mention some peculiar structures which allow us a glimpse into the difficulties which the inhabitants of this area faced due to the extremely dry climate. These structures are of great interest in regard to the previously put-forth supposition that no large populations of agricultural people could possibly have lived in this region, given the present climactic conditions.

Water from the mesa empties into the cañons below by way of smaller ravines. Built across the bottoms of these ravines, we find the barely-discernable remains of low walls, often only a short distance from one another. There can be no doubt here that we are dealing with ancient dams or water reservoirs which served to collect precipitation during the rainy season. Such reservoirs are found located above most of the ruins. One built upon a very large scale lies on the mesa, several miles north of the last-named ruins, not far from a significant rubble-pile or ruin. It is formed by a circular wall, 100 feet in diameter. A canal led to this reservoir from a nearby ravine.

I have above put forth a number of points of comparison between the Moki Indians and the people who once inhabited the Mesa Verde region. Both built houses of stone, although the art of building is considerably poorer in the case of the Moquis. Further, both peoples kept turkeys as livestock. They cultivated maize as their most important foodstuff, as well as beans and a type of pumpkin. Both wove fabric of cotton and were skillful potters, although even here a decided regression may be noted among the Moquis. Even though other regressions might also be noticed, there should be no doubt that, as has earlier been postulated, the Moki Indians are the descendents of an agricultural people spread out over a large area, to which the Mesa Verde "Cliff dwellers" also belonged.

I have here been able to touch only fleetingly upon many of the Mesa Verde region's most notable ruins and the artifacts found in them, which give us some insight into the culture of the inhabitants, their customs, and their way of life. A collection of 500 artifacts, assembled from my excavations, and a large series of photographs (150) offer rich material for a work about the ruins of the Mesa Verde region. In this book, which is soon to be published, I have had liberty to treat in greater detail the subject of this shorter discourse: the ruins of Southwestern Colorado.

1

2

3

4

5

6

7

Fig. 8. Meander Patterns

82

The development of the meander-pattern among Colorado's cliff dwellers

By G. Nordenskiöld

(Translated from *Ymer*, the annual journal of Svenska Sällskapet för Antropologi och Geografi, 1892, pp. 14-19.)

The agricultural peoples which formerly inhabited the southwestern regions of the United States, and the ruins of whose numerous dwellings are found in Arizona, New Mexico, and the bordering states, were possessed of a high degree of skill in the art of pottery-making. The earthen vessels which they produced are far superior to those made by the agricultural Indian tribes living in the same area today. This is true not only of their technique, but also of their ornamentation.

These ancient vessels have decoration in black and white colors in simple but stylistic patterns, composed almost entirely of straight lines. The modern pots, for example those of the Moki Indians, are ornamented in richer and more varied colors, but the simple, stylistic patterns have, perhaps through the influence of the white man, given way to more complicated, but tasteless and poorly drawn figures.

During my excavations carried out in the ruins of Mesa Verde, I have been able to make quite a rich collection for the study of the ornamentation found in this area (Southwestern Colorado) in particular. In my comparisons of the different ornamentations, I have often been able to observe an unbroken line of development through a series of small, unimportant changes, from simpler to more complicated patterns. The cliff dwellers had a strong tendency to copy previously used patterns down to the smallest detail. However, one may see an openness for beauty, which shows itself in the use and development of small modifications of the patterns, which in some cases might be attributed to mere coincidence, and in others to observations which the creators may have made of natural objects, or of some of the phenomena within the sphere of textiles.

In order to show the course of this development in one study, I shall refer here to a series of ornamentation, all observed on clay vessels from Mesa Verde. This series is of considerable interest,

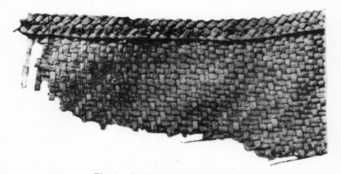

Fig. 1. Fragment af en vassmatta.

Fig. 2.

Fig. 3.

84

because it ends with use of the meander-pattern, of which so much has been written. It is my intent here to show its derivation from a simple pattern copied from the textile craft.

Fig. 1 is a mat of reeds found in a ruin in Navajo Cañon. The method of weaving used in the making of this mat is very common among the cliff dwellers. This method was also used in the making of yucca-leaf sandals. If, in weaving, one uses leaves of a darker color every other leaf, the pattern shown in fig. 8:1 will arise. I have observed not only this pattern, but also other, more complicated patterns on woven baskets, achieved through the variation of dark and light withies or leaves.[1]

The pattern in fig. 8:2 is taken from a small cylindrical mug (fig. 2). This is the same pattern as the previous one, with the exception that the white, staircase-pattern lines are separated by larger spaces. I have observed this same pattern on other vessels from Mesa Verde. This is also true of the next pattern, fig. 8:3, which developed from the former in that the ends of the white staircase patterns are connected by vertical lines. This change probably stems from a practice also taken from the weaver's craft, namely that of dividing a narrow band into quadrangular fields. Fig. 3 is a pitcher with this pattern decorating its uppermost field. Lower down, the pattern is the same, but goes in the opposite direction. In my collection, I have several vessels with the same pattern, going in one direction as well as the other. In fig. 8:4, the same pattern is seen again, this time with the exception that the separation between the different fields has been made even more pronounced by the drawing of a black line through the vertical white line itself. This pattern is to observed on the bowl in fig. 4. In fig. 8:5, the direction of the slanted, staircase-form line has been changed. Otherwise, the pattern is the same. This decoration is copied from a mug in the Wetherill's collection of pottery from Mesa Verde. I own an example of the same, although less skillfully done, on a small fragment. The next modification is shown in fig. 8:6. Here, half of the "staircase" has disappeared except for a small hook, which remains to indicate the origin of this decoration. The bowl which is depicted in fig. 5, and from which this ornamentation is taken, is a restoration according to a fragment found in a ruin in Cliff Cañon (fig. 6). Finally, fig. 8:7 shows an especially beautiful meander-pattern, derived from the last-indicated pattern only in that the points of the black lines running at right angles have now been connected. The pattern is copied from a beautiful bowl found in Spruce Tree House in Navajo Cañon (fig. 7).

I believe that I have shown above how the meander-pattern of the cliff dwellers was developed from a simple decoration taken from textiles. It is, however, not at all my intention to give the same explanation for the occurrence of this pattern among other peoples of the world. I see no reason why this ornamentation could not have arisen in several other ways. There is a great number of possible combinations of lines by which one can, with numerous small modifications, create a meander. Of these possibilities, probably quite a few have actually existed. It should be of interest to attempt to find and identify these origins, rather than to theoretically reconstruct meanders out of simpler patterns. It is this reasoning which has motivated me to publish this series of ornamentations.

---

[1]Holmes, (*U.S. Geogr. and Geol. Survey of the Territories*, 1876, p. 407) shows a portion of a mat from Mancos, with a pattern much like the one shown here.

Fig. 4.

Fig. 5.

Fig. 6.

Fig. 7.

88

An Article from the Journal

The Photographic Times

After Gustaf Nordenskiöld returned to Sweden in 1892 he worked in several fields of science. One of these was the crystallography of minerals. He combined this interest with his experience as a photographer to study snowflakes. The article which follows was published in English.

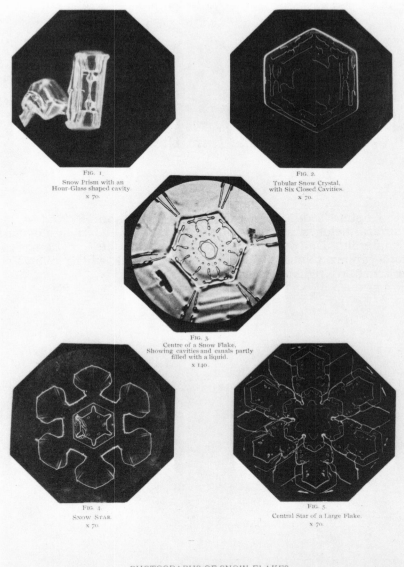

FIG. 1.
Snow Prism with an
Hour-Glass shaped cavity.
x 70.

FIG. 2.
Tubular Snow Crystal,
with Six Closed Cavities.
x 70.

FIG. 3.
Centre of a Snow Flake,
Showing cavities and canals partly
filled with a liquid.
x 140.

FIG. 4.
SNOW STAR
x 70.

FIG. 5.
Central Star of a Large Flake.
x 70.

PHOTOGRAPHS OF SNOW FLAKES,

By Prof. G. Nordenskiöld.

(ACADEMY OF SCIENCES, STOCKHOLM.)

The Photography of Snowflakes

by Prof. G. Nordenskiöld
(Academy of Sciences, Stockholm)

(*The Photographic Times*, February 1895)

The regular and beautiful form of snow stars seems always to have excited a lively interest among scientists. Olaus Magnus, the author of the celebrated *"Historia de Gentibus Septentrionalibus,"* gives in this great work, published in 1555, the first figures of snow crystals. In 1611 Kepler produced a pamphlet entitled *"Strena sen de Nive Sexangula."* In the 17th and 18th centuries a great number of papers were devoted to the description of the form and structure of snow. The most remarkable among these is that published in 1681 by Donato Rossetti, a canon of Leghorn. The figures appended to the text are more similar to *photographs* of snowflakes, and consequently more accurate than any drawings yet produced. In the present century Glaisher and Scoresby, the famous Arctic explorer, among others, have figured and described snow crystals of many different types.

It is evident that the *drawing* of a snow crystal, which so readily evaporates, or, at the slightest rise of temperature above the freezing-point, melts, must be very difficult. That nobody has ever actually succeeded in drawing a perfectly correct figure of a snowflake is clearly shown by the results of photography when employed in this department of science.

Photographs of snow crystals were first taken, to the best of my knowledge, in 1887, by Mr. Arthur W. Waters, an Englishman. In 1890 I made my first experiments in this line, but it was not until the winter of 1892-93 that I commenced my systematic endeavors to elucidate the different forms of crystallized snow. During the same winter R. Neuhaus, of Berlin, took a number of snow photographs. He, however, used low power lenses, and the most interesting details in the structure of the snow stars consequently escaped him.

I formerly used a common vertical photomicrographic camera in combination with a Siebert microscope. But for last winter's work I constructed an apparatus designed especially for snow photography (see cut). The upper part of the camera (answering to the back of an ordinary camera) is carried by four brass tubes telescoping into four tubes of the same length. By means of this arrangement the camera may be drawn out to nearly twice the length shown in the figure. Conical screws are set around the upper ends of the outer tubes and the upper part can thus be fixed at any height. The lower (front) end of the camera consists of a square board, to the corners of which are attached cylindrical set-screws fitted round the outer tube and movable along the same. The centre of the board carries a short tube, worked by a milled-head-screw, and fitting into a cap applied to the ocular end of the microscope.

The fine adjustment is simply worked by a metal rod bearing at the lower end a small wheel, round the margin of which is stretched a rubber band. The rod passes through a hole in a small elongated brass plate, which is fastened to the board at the lower end of the camera by a screw inserted through a slot in the plate. The rod and wheel can thus be moved a short distance in an horizontal direction. When the camera has been brought over the microscope, the wheel is slightly pressed, by means of this screw, against the milled screw of the fine adjustment, and the adjustment may easily be worked by turning the head of the rod.

Each of the four tubes supporting the camera rests on a circular brass foot, furnished at the bottom with a T-shaped slot. These slots run on a pair of T-shaped rails fixed to a solid table, and the whole camera may thus be moved along the table by means of a rack-and-pinion mechanism. This arrangement enables the operator in a few seconds to bring the camera into position, exactly in the axis of the microscope, a condition of great importance in the kind of work under consideration, where a delay on his part may be fatal to the result.

The manipulation of snowflake photography does not differ greatly from that observed in other classes of photomicrographic work. The difficulties consist principally in the tendency of the minute snowflakes to melt, or evaporate. When the atmospheric temperature is well below the freezing-point the melting is easily prevented by taking care not to touch the stage of the microscope or the slip of glass bearing the object with the hand.

APPARATUS EMPLOYED BY PROF. NORDENSKIOLD FOR PHOTOGRAPHING SNOW CRYSTALS.

"The Photography of Snow Flakes," *Photographic Times* (Feb. 1895), pp. 95.

At a temperature of only a few degrees below the freezing-point the work becomes very difficult, and freezing mixtures must be used to keep microscope and glass slips cold. The rapid evaporation of the snow is a more serious difficulty, and causes the operator great inconvenience. A snowflake lying free on a slip of glass will begin to lose its regular form and within a minute, or less*. A thin cover-glass does not damage it in the least, and considerably retards the evaporation. The ice vapor, however, sometimes forms spots on the glass. In my experiments the best way of obtaining a good photograph of a fine crystal is to place it quickly on a glass slip, put a small drop of a colored liquid on it and lay the cover-glass over. The liquid must, of course, have a low freezing point. I used aniline oil, in which an aniline color had been dissolved. In this liquid the most delicate star would remain entirely unaltered for hours.

The observing and photographing of snow crystals in a colored liquid is of great interest. The oil slowly penetrates into the cavities and narrow canals, which are nearly always present in a snow star or table. This is a proof that the curved lines, often very complicated (see the figures), in the interior of the crystals mark the limits of regular, flattened cavities, bounded by sinuous surfaces. In many crystals, these cavities are closed (Fig. 2). In others, especially in the star-like varieties, they take the shape of slender double canals, radiating from the centre (Fig. 3), and usually forming the middle of the six arms.

The kaleidoscopic wealth of form displayed by these figures in the interior of snowflakes renders the photographing of snow stars a very fascinating pastime. Anybody who possesses a microscope and a camera may easily construct an apparatus with which he can take good snow photographs.

---

*The snow crystals photographed by Dr. R. Neuhauss are good evidence of this. He does not seem to have paid any attention to the rapid evaporation, and he used no cover glass. The result is that nearly every star has lost the original form, which is bounded by mathematically regular straight lines, in accordance with the laws of the hexagonal system of crystals.

If the lenses are not apochromatic, orthochromatic plates and a light-filter must be used. Those who wish to give their snow photographs a scientific value should always make full meteorological observations once or twice a day so long as the work is in progress. With a large stock of such observations it might perhaps be possible to ascertain the conditions under which the different forms of crystals are generated. The north-east of the United States, with its cold winters is, no doubt, a region highly congenial to this kind of work.

(All the snowflakes shown in the figures, with the exception of Fig. 3, are photographed against a black background by using an "opaque-centre stop.")

BIBLIOGRAPHY

PUBLICATIONS BY NORDENSKIÖLD.

1. *The Cliff Dwellers of the Mesa Verde-Southwestern Colorado: Their Pottery and Implements.* Translated by D. LLoyd Morgan.
   Chicago: P. A. Norstedts & Söner Förlag, 1892
   Reprint: New York: AMS Press, 1973
   Reprint: Glorieta, New Mexico: The Rio Grande Press, 1979
   Reprint: Mesa Verde National Park, Colorado: Mesa Verde Museum Association, 1990

2. *Ruiner af klippboningar i Mesa Verde.* (Stockholm: P. A. Norstedt & Söner Förlag, 1892).

3. *Från fjärran västern: minnen från Amerika.* (*From the Far West: Memories from America),* Stockholm P. A. Norstedt & Söner Förlag, 1892).

4. "Om några märkliga ruiner i sydvestra Colorado" (On some remarkable ruins in Southwestern Colorado), *Ymer,* 1892, pp. 3-13.

5. "Om mäanderns utveckling hos Colorados klippfolk" (The development of the meander pattern among Colorado's Cliff Dwellers), *Ymer,* pp. 14-19.

6. "Om mineral från drushål vid Taberg i Vermland" (Mineral samples from the mines at Värmland), *Geologiska Föreningens Förhandlingar,* XII 203, pp. 136, 348-358.

7. "Om kentrolit och malanotekit" (A study of centrolite and malanotechite), *Geologiska Föreningens Förhandlingar,* XVI 15, p. 151-160.

8. "Spodiosit från Nordmarken" (Spodosite from Nordmarken) *Geologiska Föreningens Förhandlingar,* XV 73, pp. 415, 460-466.

9. "Analys af vesuvian (hos Widman)" (An analysis of vesuvianite (after Widman), *Geologiska Föreningens Förhandlingar*, XII 28.

10. "Om några sällsynta mineral från Igaliko i Grönland" (Some rare minerals from Igaliko in Greenland), *Geologiska Föreningens Förhandlingar*, XVI 244, pp. 246, 336-346.

11. "Preliminärt meddelande rörande en undersökning af snökristaller" (Preliminary notes from an examination of snow crystals), *Geologiska Föreningens Förhandlingar*, XV 128, (u.) 129, 146-158.

12. " Tvenne fotografier af snökristaller" (Two photographs of snow crystals), *Geologiska Föreningens Förhandlingar*, XX, pp. 163-165.

13. "Några anteckningar om fosfatlagren i Florida" (Some notes on the phosphate deposits in Florida), *Geologiska Föreningens Förhandlingar*, XIV 283, pp. 356-357.

14. "The Photography of Snow Flakes," *Photographic Times* (Feb. 1895), pp. 95-97.

RELATED PUBLICATIONS

15. Arrhenius, Olof W. *Stones Speak and Waters Sing: The Life and Works of Gustaf Nordenskiöld*. Edited and annotated by Robert H. Lister and Florence C. Lister. (Mesa Verde National Park, Colorado: Mesa Verde Museum Association, 1984).

16. Cather, Willa. *The Professor's House*, (New York: 1925).

17. "Dödsruna- G. Nordenskiöld, ledamot" (Obituary: G. Nordenskiöld, Society member), *Geologiska Föreningens Förhandlingar*, XI 115, XVII 563, pp. 639-642.

18. Nadaillac, Marquis de, Jean Francois. *L'Amérique Prehistorique*. (Paris, 1883).

19. Nadaillac, Marquis de, Jean Francois. *Pre-Historic America*. Trans. by N. D'Anvers. (New York, 1895).

20. Nordenskiöld, A. E. *The Voyage of The Vega Round Asia and Europe*. (London: Macmillan & Co., 1881).

21. Stolpe, Hjalmar. "Gustaf Nordenskiöld", *Congrés International des Américanistes, 1894* (Stockholm: Ivar Hæggström, 1897).

22. Wetherill, Benjamin Alfred. *The Wetherills of the Mesa Verde: The Autobiogphy of Benjamin Alfred Wetherill,* Ed. by Maurine S. Fletcher. (Lincoln: University of Nebraska Press, 1977).